MINNESOTA POEMS FROM THE OUTPOSTS

Hari Hyde

Copyright © 2024 by Hari Hyde

All Rights Reserved. No portion of this book may be reproduced in any form without permission from the publisher, except as permitted by U.S. copyright law.

This is a work of fiction. Names, characters, places, and incidents are either the product of the author's imagination or are used fictitiously. Any resemblance to actual persons, living or dead, events, or locales, is entirely coincidental.

ISBN (e-book): 979-8-9867181-5-6

ISBN (paperback): 979-8-9867181-6-3

Book Cover Design by ebooklaunch.com

A Minnesota poet explores the astonishing small towns, unflappable freethinkers, fanciful folklore, faithful families, and glorious watery wilderness of the North Star State.

Contents

PART I: middle rivers 1

    MIDDLE RIVER, MINNESOTA 3

    GOOSE CAPITAL 5

    YOUNG'S STORE (Middle River, MN) 9

    SCHOOL BUS 12

    MOON OVER THIEF LAKE 14

    YE OLDE DEPOT THEATRE, RIVER AVENUE 16

    IDENTITY AND SOCIETY 18

    BEASTLY STOICISM 20

    NEIGHBORS 23

    MILKING HOLSTEINS 25

    ANGUS CATTLE 28

    MINNESOTA HIGHWAY 59 30

    UNRUFFLED RAILWAY 33

    MINNESOTA HIGHWAY 32 36

    SAILING THE MIDDLE RIVER 38

    HEARTLAND RIVER 40

    SMALLTOWN BANDSTAND 42

    GARDENS 45

    MAN-SIZED MEMORIAL PARK 48

    CHURCH BELL 49

PART II: smalltown outposts.................................. 51

- MINNESOTA MAPS.. 53
- MOON OVER LAKE OF THE ISLES (MPLS, MN) 55
- GRAND MARAIS, MINNESOTA 57
- SPLIT ROCK LIGHTHOUSE (Lake Superior) 59
- MINNESOTA'S TEN MILLENNIAL GIRL 61
- BLUE MOUNDS STATE PARK 63
- WINONA BREW 64
- PAULETTE BUNYAN 66
- DINKYTOWN USED BOOK STORE 68
- ITASCA: MISSISSIPPI RIVER HEADWATERS 71
- MANKATO MAN AND NATURE'S PLAN............. 73
- MINNESOTA'S AWKWATOK.................................. 75
- MOSQUITOES AND LOONS 78
- RED RIVER FLOOD (East Grand Forks, MN) 79
- THE TIMBER HOUND 82
- LITCHFIELD, MINNESOTA BAKERY 84
- GRAND MOUND IN KOOCHICHING COUNTY 86
- SMALLTOWN BRAIN 88
- BIG BLACK BEAR STATUE (Northome, MN) 90
- FRAZEE TO OLIVIA: THE BOUNDLESS BIG 92
- THE VOYAGEURS ON PIGEON RIVER 94
- NEW YORK MILLS RAIN.. 96
- LAKE BEMIDJI GOOSE 98

PART III: inner outposts 99
- PRIVATE PONDS 101
- SECRET SNOW BONES 104
- LAST LOVE.. 107
- LAUGHTER.. 110
- RENDEZVOUS... 112
- MACHINE CHUCKLES 113
- THE BELIEVABLE DISTANCE 115
- ANCIENT APATHY.. 117
- TEETER-TOTTER 118
- BATHED BRAIN 120
- LUMBERING BRAIN... 122
- BRAIN RIVER.. 124
- GUARD DOG 125
- LAYERS... 126
- SUNLIGHT STOOPED 128
- THE IMPERSONATOR 129
- THE OUTSIDE... 131
- SALT AND SNOW 132
- UNSTILL BIRTH 133
- WIND AND MUSIC 134
- FAILURE 136

PART IV: family and faith **139**

- MINNESOTA SAINTS 141
- THE PARENT'S HOUR 144
- FATHER AND SON 146
- MOTHER AND SON 148
- MY PICTURE POSTCARD 149
- WHAT'S THE CATCH? (My Cat's Name) 151
- ELEGY FOR A NOBODY 153
- A COVEY OF CRITIQUES 157
- CORPORAL COUNSELOR 159
- ONE SOUL 164
- COLLEGE 165
- A BABY'S BIRTH 166
- AN ACT OF KINDNESS 167
- GET WELL CARDS (calibrated) 168
- JONAH AND THE GREAT FISH 172
- FAMILIES 178
- UNCLE SCHOOL 180
- BIBLE UNDERSTUDY (LUKE 23: 42–43) 182
- HIS FAMILY 185
- THE MACHINE-LEARNING FAMILY 186
- PRAY CASUALLY 187
- A LITTLE LIGHT 189

PART V: the wild **191**
- MOOSE HEAD 193
- ARROWHEAD NORTHERN LIGHTS 195
- THE WHIRLING SQUIRREL 197
- WIND IN THE NORTHLAND PINES 199
- GOPHER GRAVEYARDS 201
- MINNESOTA WILDLAND 203
- FAKE FIREFLIES 204
- BEAVERS 205
- LIGHTNING'S RETURN STROKES 207
- PEOPLE'S PRECINCTS. NATURE'S QUARTERS 208
- INTO THE WOODS 210
- THE CLAN OF SILENCE 224
- LAKE OF THE WOODS 226
- SNOW PLANET 236
- BOUNDARY WATERS CANOE AREA, MINNESOTA 239
- ABOUT THE AUTHOR 241

PART I:
middle rivers

MIDDLE RIVER, MINNESOTA

America's little rivers rush, then rest,
enabling and entrusting big rivers to race
in a juggernaut's unstoppable pace,
ceaselessly slogging an incessant quest.

Minnesota's Middle River marches in spring.
Up north, this watercourse hastens toward June,
murmuring, sprinkling, and tinkling its tune.
September salvages mud-laden pools that cling

to spring. The riverbed bares a cracked mire.
Boots stroll a dry bottom where torrents once played.
Leafy litter remains from this creek's cavalcade,
recasting July's empire in soiled attire.

Middle River royally parcels its name—
to title a town, to christen its water!
Which half is the father? Which one the daughter?
The duo, like heartbeats, flickers in fame.

Middle River, the first, serves as a harbor for home.
Middle River, the other, rolls as a haven for mud.
As both a fleeting, fugitive flood
and a rural farming land's dome,

two middle rivers tally the sum
embodying the rapturous rhythms of life.

Another season will spring to remedy strife.
Tomorrow trumpets when adversities drum.

By autumn, the Middle River empties its hose.
Just so, this river town relinquishes kids,
seeking fortune forecasted in Big River's grids,
but lugging more luggage than any suppose.

Winters require a river's repose,
in a season when memories stir,
and flashes of hindsight occur.
By springtime, remembrance flows.

For grads with diplomas, sentimentality froze,
but flashbacks of childhood, like rivers, resurge.
Reminders of smalltown schooldays emerge.
The boat's skipper steers. A memory rows.

GOOSE CAPITAL

Their squadron scissored the moon.
A gust of geese cleaved the night
as a torrent of hoots hurtled
down from the cacophonous choir.
This dancing dagger of flapped feathers
splintered the curtain of tumbling rain.
The hunt for wayfaring gaggles
haunted my wiles, provoking my quest.
Once honked upon, one wishes
to harvest the honk. My passions

played in the firmament's fairyland.
I arose to invade the aerial realms.
From my pellets, they'll plummet
to replenish my belly, grown fat,
yet not as fatty as goose breast,
the fattiest meat ever hatched.
Hunters of fowl ply dexterity,
as jack of all trades, master of one,
the gatherer of ganders and dames,
the gaggle of wings from the clouds.

To hunt, one must scout. One must
think like a goose, discover the fields
where they feed, mark their motives

for conspiring to rob one farmer's field,
neglecting the cropland of his neighbor.
To hunt, one must hoax and seduce
the shrewdest goose, the savviest fowl,
the canniest bird, more astute than us all.
I sculptured my decoys, whittled and hewn
and painted, but not with a gloss that a goose

would mock as the banal bric-a-brac of men,
intended to hoodwink them to visit their kin.
My decoys twinned the facade of a goose
as much as my mirror casts a facsimile of me.
Condone their pride, for a goose promenades
as an aristocrat, wearing a tailcoat and cravat
in a white-tie affair—a pose, then a stiff strut.
To hunt, one must hide, and husks of a cornfield
masked me from aery surveillance. In shrouds,
I lay camouflaged from the voyeurs of the skies.

To hunt, one must tootle the most hypnotic oboe
that ever dazzled a theater of finicky flocks.
Men can be netted, rather easily deceived,
but geese are the most circumspect foe,
suspicious, vigilant, watchful, and wise.
Past misadventures foretell of danger below.
I rehearsed like a kazoo virtuoso, awaiting
opening night's risen curtain, until certain
my single-reed pipe clucks and moans
every salutation of convivial waterfowl.

Announced by sky-high, brash buglers,
they arrive, the babel of pandemonium's kites,
a bedlam of wings. Yet jubilance springs
as the flock circles, lower and lower,
above my mannikins, my taciturn dolls.
Squeezing melodious moans from my reed,
I avoided a common rookie mistake.
To hunt, one must beseech loudest
when the prey flaps an inch from your face.
Firecrackers leapt from five hunters' wands,

launched from my crew's ambuscade.
When geese fall, they dive beyond doubt,
plunging fast, with not one wing holding out,
as bold as their birth, still game in their end.
I felt my innermost phantoms incandesce,
as though I wrested their secretive specters
to flock in my remembrance forever.
Winged wildness hovers as a benevolent beast,
a holy soul, a galvanizing ghost of our feast.
Stripped of our feathers, we dined as bedfellows.

Some nights, when a flock ferries the moon
and the babble of beaks startles the sky,
a convocation of encircling memories alights,
reminiscences of the scouting, the hoaxing,
the hiding, the tootling, and the beseeching.
Then I gently hum a honk on my musical reed,
and I fancy my wishes could summon a realm,

unseen by us stalkers, known only to geese.
As I piped, an approaching image grew taller,
a curious hunter, another meat caller.

YOUNG'S STORE (MIDDLE RIVER, MN)

Overflowing, brimming, packed,
like a galaxy's smorgasbord of stars,
this store arose staggeringly stacked,
resembling ancient, ebullient bazaars,
with aisles as filled as railroad cars.

Why only buy a thing or three?
The universe awaits herein.
Initiate a shopping spree.
Let acquisitional quests begin.
Explore each shelf, each alley, each bin.

Age-old emblem of this small town's pride,
Young's General Store yet captivates
each customer, each child, wide-eyed,
who burrows through the magical gates,
where a treasure trove proliferates.

If your heart desires it,
and your head does too,
Mister Young requires it
to be instore or overdue,
as his inventory grew.

For farmers, hunters, handymen,
find clothing, hardware, cookeries,

and toys enough for Santa's den,
a king's kitchenful of groceries,
and the stuff that runs on batteries.

Inquire of Mister Young, "Say,
have you a cowboy hat in stock?"
— "I do," he'll reply. "Sold one today."
"And I will need two bicycle locks."
— "Aisle four, atop of the clocks."

"And I need a tinted windowpane."
— "My backroom's where I harbor glass."
"Got any gauge that measures rain?"
— "Got one for the roof. Got one for the grass."
"Fantastic find! What mounds, you amass!

But … I'll stump you yet. Pink birthday candles?"
— "Which size? The smaller ones work fine."
"Wrought iron pitcher pumping handles?"
— "Just arrived. A shipment of nine,
with pipes enough for an Alaskan pipeline."

"Try this! A jet-propelled space rocket
that flies to Mars on a weekend trip?"
— "Got one right here in my jacket pocket,
the order slip, I mean. I'll soon equip
the store with your futuristic Martian ship."

"I'm thunderstruck. This general store
must be where every adventurer shops,

the one and only shop, safaris now explore.
Glorious goods, heaped to the treetops,
alight at your site, as lavishly as raindrops.

Yet, tell me: What one item do you still lack?"
— "Friend, I've sought but one rare entry more,
something not wrapped in a sack.
You added it a few heartbeats before,
the moment you stepped into our store."

SCHOOL BUS

Gravel roads boxed up a square mile
of Spruce Valley Township where
their farm nestled like a flower bed
in a rock-rimmed garden. It's Monday,
early morning, but looks like late night.
An orange bus, seemingly a runaway
from the tardy sunrise, creeps across
the horizon, just above a farm field,
moving right to left, never up. But
for two boys, this school bus burns
impetuously, inciting expectancy
of endurable dangers, of fortuitous
friends and foes, of fledgling
scholarship, rediscoveries of dogma,

another expedition into wits' wilderness.
Though school walls stand lusterless,
this orange bus hastens to confront them.
Their plights will collide in coordinates of time.
They imagine that they strode into the belly
of a beast and survived. The bus blazes
like a galloping wildfire, the morning's torch,
gone long before the languorous sun arises.
One boy will jump off and on the bus at railroad

tracks, to wave the bus onward. "All is clear."
It's always clear. The boys time their frantic

sprint up the stretching, sandy driveway when
the bus draws closer. They never arrive at the road
sooner than the bus. That delirious dash somehow
escalates the thrill of their roadside rendezvous.
Their mother watches her boys catapult onto the bus.
She's hanging wildly flapping laundry on the
clothesline in a brutal breeze. The oaks' autumn
leaves hiss, "Yessssss." The snaps of the laundry
bark, "No!" A pillow sheet slips off one clothespin
and undulates half-heartedly, like a boy's bandana
nodding acquiescence and bidding youth farewell.

MOON OVER THIEF LAKE

Across Thief Lake, atop its rippling plane,
a wrinkling yellow ribbon, moonlight's track,
lured wanderers to walk its liquid lane.

A dreamer entered, glancing back
at shrouded woods, bereft of lustrous gloss.
Her footfalls trod above the twinkling aisle.

The splashes spattered water. She swam across,
deceived, inveigled, fooled by moonlight's guile.
The moon, adrift, still levitated

among the firmament's marauding spheres.
Its orbit nevermore accelerated,
nor slowed to peer and preen in Thief Lake's mirrors,

until this hallowed night when moonlight lodged
within these dimpled dents, this looking glass,
which sought the signs that other waters dodged.

Bewitched, the moon delayed. The galaxy's morass
relinquished ownership of lunar land,
emancipating moonlight, freed, released

from lighthouse duties, from night's command.
This eve, the moon's itinerary ceased.
Adieu! to Earth's revolving satellite.

The moon gazer swam to greet
her paramour, her astral kite, the lunar sprite,
who leapt and plunged at least one billion feet.

But thieves abscond with hearts for thieving's sake.
Alas, the dreamer's grave mistake
befell when moonquakes raged around Thief Lake.

YE OLDE DEPOT THEATRE, RIVER AVENUE

Theater twinkles, when local,
when the playhouse sprouts
an orchard of organic plots

and amateur actors portraying
a second self, a deputy psyche,
a beloved imposter whom everyone

knows bears an improbable,
though not impossible, resemblance
to these neighborhood natives.

When a farming community sows
the seeds of a theatrical garden,
a smalltown oasis, amidst acres

of wheat, oats, and sunflower fields,
a little Eden germinates. The lifeblood
of vegetable beds metamorphose

into trustworthy thespians, genuine
translators of print on the page.
You know them on-and-off of the stage.

This smalltown arena arose
from a refurbished railway depot,
a station wherein personas perform

tales of adventurous episodes,
like and unlike the lives of anyone here.
How actors must hesitate to recite

their lines! "I've never said this before,
but I've heard these words somewhere,
wandering imaginative minds, maybe mine."

Enlist local children into the cast of performers
of offbeat fairy tales. Magical mayhem
alights on the audience, the senior oldsters

and parents, delighting in bizarre dialogues.
Mom and Pop laugh, as venerable veterans
laugh, chuckling at life's fun-loving fiascos.

Child actors feel strange, dispatching their lines.
Words feel like a truth and a lie. In stage whispers,
their parents hoot: *Now you know how we felt.*

IDENTITY AND SOCIETY

A town, a farm, one mile apart, occurred
as Earth and moon, a split society,
that set the stage, the theater, for Ray,

a farmer's boy, a teenage man-child, stirred
by cryptic queries, by curiosity
on matters rigged to rouse a runaway.

Aglow, the meager lights from town inferred
communal comforts, fond felicity,
a blush atop the farmyard's stack of hay,

a quilt across the sleeping cattle herd.
Then moonlight questioned Ray's identity.
The moon assumed Ray's jubilation lay

in solitude, those monologues that spurred
the moon to hover high, in majesty,
a mirror that meditates, escorting day.

Be like the moon: alone, an isle, assured
of flashy individuality,
of rare peculiarity, a stray,

a maverick among the herd—*that* word
will mean monotonous conformity.
Remain aloof as crows, where cornfields sway.

Be one, the free. Not two, just me. And third,
be he who disregards posterity.
Withdraw, *adieu!* to men. Let moonrise stay.

The village glow emerged inane, absurd.
Then Ray recalled his past proclivity
for gripping games that frisky fellows play.

And streetlights shone as though a hue preferred
to lunar light. The luminosity
of Jane arose. Folks call her Missus Ray.

BEASTLY STOICISM

Asleep in my farmhouse,
away from the work,
I floated in the olden sea.
Then a booming bellow
wrenched me awake.
A melee in the barn,
two creatures quarreling,
sought an audience.
Not costumed for rain,
I launched out of the house,

with only a flashlight to wrestle
the raindrops. The linear beam
bounced off the wild water,
and my halo sparkled,
as though I were a jewel.
I spied stoic sparrows,
lined up on a power line cable,
next to the yard light,
like the next train to Heaven,
and I waved my dazzling wand

toward them, just to force their reaction.
They seemed mildly interested
but found the scene unremarkable.

When I tripped over some lumber
I'd intended to move yesterday,
my splash and blaspheming
rattled the backbone of the night.
But the birds reckoned the rain
bestowed a more apropos show,
and they puffed up their feathers

to escape to that olden sea, I'd departed.
Past a pause, I crept into the barn,
where the brawl had already ended, when
my pregnant prize cow dropped her calf,
who flopped around, attempting
to get on her feet, looking wetter than me,
even though I'm the one braving the rain.
My boot slipped on the afterbirth.
Mother's neck turned, secure in her stanchion,
and she looked back at me.

She looked so subtly, softly inquisitive,
almost a compassionate glance,
as though pondering why anyone
could fancy the episode paramount
among the entirety of existence.
A farm cat on the barn rafters
stared at me, not the cow, not the calf,
presumably wondering about my usual
overreaction this time, just like every time
before this. She's already forgotten

about her kittens she nurtured one week ago.
I helped the calf to her hoofs and stuck
my index finger in her mouth to shut her up,
and she started sucking my fingernail dry.
I filled up a milk pail, the one with the nipple,
and soon she grew utterly contented.
Whenever I sat in a church pew, I'd sought
this forbearance, endurance, which only beasts
attain. They take things as they come. Among
myriad paths, be ever grateful for traveling one.

NEIGHBORS

When cattle herds break through their fence,
I stop to wonder why.
Do cattle seek immense events,
as dazed as you or I?

One cow gazes now, but hesitates.
She gapes erratically
at sagging wires and meditates
on immortality.

Then gingerly, the cow advances.
Emancipation's gate
awaits for gamblers taking chances.
Eleven cows vacate

the pasture, seeking who-knows-what,
a lusher land, a beach
of sanctuary. Cattle strut
toward raptures out of reach.

In single file, the herd patrols
the crackling gravel road.
Though ditches offer greener holes,
and gravel can't be mowed,

they wish to stride where autos strode,
this avenue of stones.

The road forebodes an episode
through adventitious zones.

My neighbor's truck confronts the herd
and stops, a yard from harm.
Without a bawl or bovine word,
returning to the farm,

the herd retraces paces past,
back through the broken fence.
Their misadventure proves the last
attempt at impudence.

Thank neighbors' animosities
toward avaricious hordes
for reinstating boundaries
that vigilance affords.

MILKING HOLSTEINS

At the far edge of the pasture, the black
and white mottled coats of the Holstein
herd suggest an artist's brush sought
to concoct camouflage, perhaps to conceal
them from me, someone whose realm stays
in gradations of gray. The stark separation
of color-consummate white and color-vacuous
black startles me, and I wonder if everything
in the world is that simple and obvious,
and everyone knows this except me.
Each evening, we reenact our theatrical trek.

They surely know I've arrived to drive them
back to the barn for their milking. Each time,
they stare at me, as though I've decided
to alter the agenda today. A cow plunges her neck
down twice to snatch grass, then glares at me,
not happy nor sad, maybe trying to remember why
my presence signifies something urgent. I feel
like I'm expected to explain myself. This time,
the herd is standing in huge puddles, left by the rain.
They know the water serves as a moat. I won't wade
in the water without rubber boots. So I yell and throw

turf in their impermanent pond. The splashes signal
I mean business. Finally, they move at a languorous
pace toward the barn, tails switching, some cryptic
salute directed at me. One by one, they walk through
the barndoor. Each cow remembers exactly which
stanchion I've assigned to her neck, like a schoolgirl's
stroll to her personal desk. They know more than they
let on. I clean their udders with warm water. I clutch
two teats in two hands and extract a white elixir.
Milky squirts collide with the metal pail, sounding

like the labored breaths of a galaxy. I smell milk
and manure, and I love their composite bouquet.
The smell of milk carries a sense of beginning,
an intense blooming, an unruly wrenching. The smell
of manure gestures as the interim of all things, not a
halt, but a hesitation, an abundant interlude wherein
we know more will occur. That amalgam of milk and
manure elicits the ferocious emotions that roil in the
rubric of my grand transience. The too-tame barn cats
twiddle their tails, knowing we engage in the good.

My forehead rests on the cow's rumbling belly,
and I milk as an obedient machine. My arms seesaw
like knocks from a clock. We, she and I, got trained
in our callings. We're serene and thankful, gratified
that we've entered contentment. The Holstein stares
ahead, munching on feed, seeing something not there,
an invisible realm where these acts truly happen. I

clutch tenaciously her udder's outlandish spouts, as though grasping a lifeline, for I'm starting to see what she sees.

ANGUS CATTLE

Legal immigrants, the beast and I,
found fortune while gathered in a herd.
I stood in my pasture, creature to creature,
in a mutual stare with my Black Angus cow.
She parked patiently, expecting to win
our stare-down, but then plunged her head
to rip a grass salad. Insightful about small
matters, the cow fostered no fear, nor curiosity,
nor pondering. She surmised I'd neither enhance
nor remove her food options at this moment.

Instead, I knew she weighed my core worth,
my capacity to afford an amusing diversion,
an opened door to a new facet of her world
that could revitalize her memory of calfhood,
an enigma, an inscrutable mystery. Our ancestors
arrived on separate boats from Scotland,
a century ago. Our great-grandparents endured
appalling hardships, perhaps with less forethought
about our present generation than we might fancy.
But now, we two share a pasture in momentary bliss,

those ephemeral hours of serenity when life loiters,
conniving to perch us atop the highest pedestal
before the nosedive. I named this cow "Angie." I know

every name in my herd. I've wondered if each cow
selects a different name for me. I herd carcass cattle,
a mountain of meat, life after death. Cattle and humans
rank as the most prevalent mammals on Earth. Flavorful
and tender, Angus muscle is marbled with fat.
As herbivores, Angus never discovered they taste good.
No horns sprout from an Angus. They can walk soon

after birth and breed a year later, life in a hurry,
less time to worry. Angie regurgitates her cud,
chewing her entree again, and relishing the revival
of the grass that sprouted anew in her stomach
as miraculous manna, wholly unexpected, but no more
than she deserves. Angie seems to know that she
possesses a purpose. She lives one day at a time.
Though I've attained no intrinsic utility, I invent
abstract objectives. Angie and her kin survive
solely as edible ambassadors. I feast to safeguard
the birthright of these glorious beasts.

MINNESOTA HIGHWAY 59

A man at seventeen, he dreamed
of escapades, mounting Highway 59
to Mexico or Canada.
This road retains its two digits,
until another nation's border intervenes.

For years, he'd strolled along this byway,
his getaway's tinseled tar.
Escapeways wave alluringly
to yardbirds, captives one and all,
retaining one pose in a picture frame too long.

But Mexico and Canada,
surprisingly, failed to freshen
his skull's stratosphere,
as though new nations tried to conceal
novelties from him.

Lake Winnipeg hid its fish,
just as Rainy Lake would do,
till a fishing rod's rescue
reveals the same invisible prowlers
swim in the same borderless, unsalted sea.

Nuevo Laredo tamales tasted the same.
The eyes of Mexican locals futilely

sought his identity, in cursory glances,
just as American stares had fruitlessly
brushed the crust of his selfhood, his singularity.

He thought his wrapped essence would unravel
in alien eyes. But their gazes arrived
from the same strange distance, where everyone
he'd known must reside. He stood as a stranger.
Their cordiality and hospitality felt so odd.

Maybe aggression could better allow us to connect
as decipherable creatures protecting our nests.
At the first instant, foreign words, alien objects,
suggested a new lawless language,
pledging to fracture the fence corralling our minds.

But the bright images accentuated
his aloneness, his incessant solitude.
Tinkling margarita glasses
clinked to announce tiny cracks
in the unseen barricade,

but the wall never topples,
nor opens its gate.
He roamed as a quarantined explorer,
a pioneer prevented from entry,
witnessing a pantomime of his life.

Each life replays on a stage,
a theater adrift in your skull,

its railings irrevocable,
its cellblock locked, evermore.
Escape, but bring your castle along.

UNRUFFLED RAILWAY

Alongside Highway 32, a railway stretches side by side
this motorway by Middle River. The two arteries spring
as arrows, divided by a ditch. As my pickup truck
traversed through my tiny town, I slowed its gait
to ponder this anchored avenue journeying
parallel to me, as though it sought to shepherd me,
as steely chaperone. No train rolled across my sight
this hour, nor hours close behind. I thought I'd walk
upon the deserted tracks to see what I might find.
I spied bits of grain, and shards of seeds,
and beet sugar's residue. I glimpsed specks of coal
and fertilizer tossed atop some livestock feed.

Commerce rolled atop this railway, though maybe
not this week. This railway writes its own itinerary
for punctuality. The train's never late, never early.
Only passengers are ill-timed, dawdling, or hasty.
Two bright steel rails raced astride a path
into remote horizons, till the gap between
the twinned rails converged upon one point,
before they reached the limits of my sight.
The ancient timber ties lay weathered.
Their complexions matched the crushed stones,
clattering below. But this railway ferries memories

of a small town's history. And a ghostly locomotive
tugs its crowded cars of memoirs. These tracks
escort the archives of souls who sailed from here,
unspooling the heartstrings that ushered their hopes.

Railways tote emotion in unforeseen,
mythological fashion. On steel wheels,
trains trek ensconced in romantic lore,
while automobiles do not.
Trains' allure feels magical, chiefly
because their trails conform to rails.
Some say sea and sky unfurl enchanting roads,
on infinite thoroughfares. There, no route prevails,
and chaos is confessed. But all balladeers
link syllables, from locomotive to caboose,
upon tracks already laid, on aged avenues,
watching for the travelers, with impatient whistles
wailing to behold the flashing red lights throb.
A small town's souls entrain to roam
along this railway and ride the rigid rails
of history, whose writ cannot be changed.

Railroad tracks resemble life's ladder, hidden
in our cells. DNA flaunts two streaming strands,
two strings tethered by innumerable ties. DNA
sleeps until duty calls it to board more riders.
Life emanates from two naked threads,
two ancient rails, two mirrored twins. Railways
roll out across the heartland, tracing the paths

of pioneers, the parallel dreams of life's dyads.
Devout duos, wedded pairs, two rails,
two legs, two arms, each companion
confirms, not duplicates, the ties that bind us
to the journey ahead. I strolled along primeval rails,

tracks evermore arising. The train tracks served
as my frontier sidewalk. Looking neither left nor right,
I gazed straight ahead till I spied the phantom
locomotive barreling toward me. This ghostly engine
towed a chain of train cars, flowing right through me.
A rattling boxcar carried crates of childhood laughter.
A clattering flatbed ferried drums of parental love.
A grand gondola toted bins of sacred hymns.
One raucous hopper car carted my boyhood pals.
One tanker car conveyed the kindness of my neighbors.
A coil car hauled joy. No graffiti marred its side.
I never saw the engineer, the train's renowned recluse,
but when the last car beckoned, I boarded his caboose.

MINNESOTA HIGHWAY 32

Highway 32 rolls its gray banner,
numbering the boldest year of a man.
At age thirty-two, my pickup truck and I pass
eighty, in our velocity, and in thousands
of miles for her, after the odometer rollover.

The sun's at our back and we're chasing
our shadow down this motorway, unfolding
ahead. I cruise as a castaway. No traffic
encroaches my solitude, and this rural artery
relinquishes its river to me, to my reverie.

I lodge as sole tenant of a vacancy,
the gap across the launch and the landing
of life. On the horizon's fringe, the white sails
of clouds bounce on the rims of this river,
awaiting our rendezvous, somewhere out there.

A blue canopy masquerades as the dome
of my relentless gray trail. Blueness dodges.
Gray grants the genuine. Nothing tangible
abides as blue. No high-flying bird discovered
any blue sprites in the sky. My truck treks atop

yellow dashes floating on a canal. My two-way
avenue goes one-way now. Ditches ever border

life's lanes. In legal adventures, ditches get dug.
Ditches dare us to drift from the ethical path.
Horizons coax us to suspend the inevitable.

I open the truck window a crack. Wind wishes
to invade my jalopy, howling for entry. I smell
farmland's bouquet, the battalion of grains,
the black furrows gashed by a plow. Wires
on utility poles race on a parallel track,

forever ahead, never behind. They patrol
this route as my scout. One witless signpost
proclaims a speed limit for my torrent, hurling
my life's bloom, from ripeness to remnants.
Birch and spruce convene on the shores

of my cascade, a ragged, winter-worn audience
half-bored by my journey from here on to there.
Huge cylindrical hay bales sleep in a field
like wedding cakes gone bad. Afar, a farm's silo
thrusts itself heavenward as a foreboding finger,

admonishing me to seek our sacred byway above,
as a harbinger buoy, as a lighthouse to warn me
of rapids and white water ahead. But my anchorage
awaits upon the horizon, at the delta of Highway 32,
on my irrevocable route to unshakable lakes.

SAILING THE MIDDLE RIVER

None sail the Middle River,
no, not one.
Though her ripples shiver

in the sun,
her bottom sleeps right below,
as an untraveled road.

Newly born from the snow,
this fugitive flowed,
both brevity's brand

and eternity's tether,
splitting and knitting the land
in mercurial weather.

Middle River glides
through your dreams
as scenery slides

and the hourglass streams.
Wide in the spring,
narrow in fall,

she's wild as a kite on a string,
and benign as the bounce of a ball.
All waterways meet at a middle.

Aspirations drift to the centermost goal.
No one will unravel the riddle
of the river arisen from our reasoning's hole.

HEARTLAND RIVER

The Heartland River gashes a scratch
down America's breastbone, an unceasing slash,
evermore digging down along its indigenous path.

Its miraculous dagger carves strokes
that flow unidirectionally. Its blade ever gropes
northmost to southmost, unlike to-and-fro boats.

The Mississippi River drains a nation and totes
water, much as clouds ferry a stratosphere's troves
of sky's oceans, which, when unfrozen, tumble below.

Obstinate islands speckle the river, demanding land
replace this rippling string, whose knots never last.
Perpetual blinks smooth the wrinkles in its lather.

A highway for commerce, a flyway for fowl, chained
by locks, dams, and levees—this barge canal was chased
from freedom to fiefdom, once careening, now caged.

A big river ever schemes to embellish, to inflate fame
and legends. By Bena, Lake Winnibigoshish feigns
to assemble a sea from a stream, a vainglorious phase

all adolescent rivers display. At eleven miles wide,
though crawling at one mile per hour, and snow white
in winter's annual freeze, wide water poses as wise.

Our Heartland River brands itself as America's marrow, midriff, center, and core, a halfway hop to tomorrow, but wee middle rivers fill the big burrow's furrow.

SMALLTOWN BANDSTAND

Crafted by amateur carpenters, the bandstand
perched across from the post office
on Hill Avenue. School kids scythed down
an empty lot's weeds, and folks donated
lumber to erect the rough-and-ready platform.

On Saturday nights, the high school band
performed to an audience of a few dozen
family and friends, who brought their own chairs
or sat in their parked cars by the sidewalk.
Green grass peeked through the fractured cement.

The band played the notes on the sheet music.
The band started to play when the director's baton
descended, then kept pace with the rhythmic waves
of his swaying forearm. Four beats per measure
and every quarter note gets one beat, unless waltzes

pranced in three-quarter time, or a 2/4-time signature
paved the way for a polka. The dot and plain stem
of a quarter note ensured one-fourth the time
of a whole note. The treble clef featured five lines,
every time. B-flat meant B-flat. Double bar at the end.

In the dreary orthodoxy of big cities, musicians fancy
they're daring, dashing, bohemian trailblazers

who evade musical conventions, who fancy difference
denotes a meaningful advance in musicality.
But no new noise can negate the soul-crushing

congestion of city swarm. You're one loose thread
in the straightjacket, a grain of sea salt upon rice,
a feather festooning a mountain of rags. One
smothering glance at a towering high-rise throttles
any attempt at invention or a leap to an elsewhere.

In America's heartland, around her small towns,
Nature innovates. In groundbreaking glory,
this Pioneer proposes every melodic contrivance,
casting life's shifting tempos and soaring crescendos.
Nature's music thunders and whispers the future,

the monstrous beauty, each nuance of color, meaning,
and feeling. Subtlety surfaces like a sunset's palette
of chaotic colors. Nature bids her children to enroll
on her theatrical stage, not knowing the script
in advance, as avant-garde artists, as daredevils,

as instruments, construing, rendering, revising,
decoding, transposing, rewriting, embellishing,
untangling, unmasking, revealing, announcing,
an unforeseen forte, a startling pianissimo,
a ruinous sforzando, a dire diminuendo.

They live on the edge of contingencies. Each day
demands the genius of flowering brain flashes.

Will winds flatten my wheat field? Will floods bury
my farmland again? Will the livestock survive winter?
Will the road get snowplowed before I give birth?

Precarious risks arise, musically, thrillingly fresh.
But around this smalltown bandstand, residents
revere their birthright, their legacy, their fortune,
in concert with Nature. The band plays the notes.
When done, horns in parked pickup trucks honk.

GARDENS

Our farm maintained your enormous garden,
a park we'd planted just for you,
on two hundred acres. Only oats

arose in your biscuit-colored campus,
a field of sagging seeds on swaying flagpoles,
a nationality of hoary conformity.

We never sampled your mortuary grain,
the ready-to-harvest oval oats cadavers,
the relics of their arising from slow-motion,

freakish phenomena that hoisted the planted,
inert nubs up from the earth to resuscitate,
row-by-row, the melodrama: same stage, new season.

Grassy shorelines circle your sea of monotony.
Grasshoppers feast on your cornucopia.
Gopher mounds announce the residence

of rodents in your gargantuan garden.
We've killed quite a few green bugs and gophers,
though we never ate them or what they ate.

Unknown to you, we've concealed a private garden,
a magical oasis, a paradisal hideaway,
a seraphic sanctum, where glorious entrees

emerge, eager, even anxious, to satisfy our wishes,
as delightful dishes, salads, side orders, sometimes
pies. Rain or shine, they stretch out to be mine.

Snap peapods dangle their delicacy. The green
envelopes wrap lush spheres of the soil's vitality.
Potatoes play as layabouts, camouflaged in brown,

as though too modest, maybe shy, to brandish
their royalty, their dominance on dinner plates.
Their subtle, slippery granules melt on our tongues.

Beets still bleed a ruby wine. Cucumbers
smell like newness, a fragrant brightness,
a bittersweet nostalgia. Carrots, orange

railroad spikes with streaming green tresses,
bestow an aroma so perfectly mimicking
their taste, you might chew upon the vapors.

I'd pair green beans with radishes to tempt a sentry
guarding Heaven's gate, impersonating peppers' hues
and taste, as well, the sum of scents amalgamated.

Rhubarb reigns as our garden's queen. Tart
as sauerkraut until sugar, butter, and vanilla
mingle, then bloom, in the planet's perfect pie.

Our farm dog guards our garden's jewels. No deer
or rodent ever breached the fence posts of his teeth.
Even insects stay away, as though this hallowed ground

glows with piety, a precinct the spiked and spineless shun. Sometimes, I wonder whether vermin regard righteous vegetables as inconvenient weeds.

At harvesttime, your garden's stored in metal silos, till powdered for your gruel. We saved our precious garden for ourselves. You're not our dinner guests.

Everybody, everywhere, works at selling something, but priceless, cherished treasure's not for sale. Everybody sees it, but none will say they know.

MAN-SIZED MEMORIAL PARK

The smalltown corner lot hoisted a lone soldier,
a helmeted statue, clutching a downturned gun.
Flags fluttered the affairs of nation, of state,
of the missing ones, a father, a husband, a son.

This man-sized Memorial Park feels larger
than the sum of an army's infantry corps.
A brigade brandishes a concept. A battalion
battles en masse. This least soldier forswore

personal gain, while we sought aggrandizement
while sheltered, as he shouldered our share
of the duty to defend sacrosanct freedom.
Aware, he cared. What we dodge, he dared.

Feel the flash of the enormity of what he did,
on behalf of family, all of us. Faraway, over there,
he pondered the cryptic conundrum of war.
We stood—he thinking, I thanking—partners in prayer.

CHURCH BELL

The village church uplifted chimes
from peals of one angelic bell.
Through misery and jolly times,
celestial ringing bids farewell
to yesterdays that now foretell

enduring faith and fealty
to God's immortal neighborhood.
The mouths of bells stretch utterly.
No ring arrives misunderstood,
when bells retell what tattlers should.

Not quiet like a uvula,
the clapper manifests a tongue.
Seesawing like a spatula,
it's hung so bulletins get rung.
The note arrives, so old, still young.

Reverberations rattle 'round
the tiny village square. Somewhere,
a family of farmers found
in knelling bells, a prince, a prayer,
a savior sprung from over there.

As bells befit simplicity,
all families uncomplicate

their shared peculiarity,
when Sunday sermons validate
the other side of Heaven's gate.

No teeth, arrears of rounded lips,
amend the bell's angelic song.
In families, in fellowships,
a bell, oft hidden, comes along.
Unsought, bells know where bells belong.

PART II:
smalltown outposts

MINNESOTA MAPS

Maps sketch a wish, a fancy, a hope,
to corral all the space you can rope.

Cartographers assume countless coordinates
might coexist, none above its subordinates.

I depend upon you to pinpoint my station,
a house in a town in a state in a nation.

But real places perch either monstrously big
or unknowably small. No contraption can dig

up through the cosmos or down under
the photon's veneer or electricity's thunder.

What's that stuff under the stuff? I ponder.
What's that stuff atop of the stuff? No responder.

No X-ray or magnet or brain-mapping tool
can ever determine why I act like a fool.

My mind resembles amorphous, itinerant clouds,
never spotting the seed each ice crystal enshrouds.

What fish ever fancies it belongs to one flask
of wandering water that never bothers to ask

permission to mingle with the sum of the lake?
Water reneges on each slippery handshake.

Sioux and Ojibwe clashed over marks on the charts.
Friendship ends when ownership starts.

French fur traders sketched maps of a watery place.
Northwest Territory, Louisiana Purchase, by grace

of merciful God, evolved into a tolerable state
of equilibrium, as provisional maps illustrate.

Between debut and death, drifting uncharted gaps,
we're roosting in wrinkles of impalpable maps.

MOON OVER LAKE OF THE ISLES (MPLS, MN)

The moon crouched low to scatter sparks
upon the lake, the glinting marks
of scintillating acolytes,
the throbbing flock of twilight sprites.

The twinkles testified to Time,
sublimely cast in pantomime
of earthly brevity. Each sparkle winks
in jest, burlesquing mortal blinks.

An isle, reclusive, much like me,
commiserates, created free
of loyalty to lunar fates
bequeathed beyond celestial gates.

How oft the moon accosted June,
in garish, glittering festoon,
igniting Lake of the Isles's fond fire
in spangles, scintillant attire

that masquerades as starry rays.
Find gloom amid the Queen-Moon's gaze,
a stoic frozen gape, a dare
to ogling mortals. None outstare

her rigid countenance, her face,
impassively affixed in space.
Amid her twilight trek, she peers
at Lake of the Isles, then disappears

in Heaven's den, a devotee
of staid responsibility
to rote, in orbiting a lake.
She sleeps coequally awake.

Yet find her flecks of friskiness
in Lake of the Isles's acute caress
of moon confetti. She's unmasked!
She'll flash her wilder side, if asked.

GRAND MARAIS, MINNESOTA

Spend an eve in Grand Marais, my way.
The prudent prowl this tourist town by day,
when phantasmal water wraiths still hide
till moonlight sails upon their spangled side.

No fiery death more madly howls
than does sunset in Lake Superior's bowels.
Marais's wee streetlights tinkle tiny tunes
to add, past daylight's bath, their tablespoons.

A gull atop the lighthouse groans
at vanishing rocks, ones he thought he owns.
An unseen radiance in evening gloom
emerges now, among the nightfall's bleak costume.

Grand phantoms stroll the shore,
explorers from the yore of fond forevermore.
Night sprites alight, known mainly by your nose,
intangible lake pixies. Each stealthily tiptoes.

An ethereal merger of celestial scents,
from freshwater fumes, from primordial pageants,
accosts a twilight's traveler. Beguiling bouquets
of splashing mermaids betray hushed hideaways.

Moon's carpet crosses the lake's chaotic calm,
a summons from Superior, a secular psalm.
Marais will pledge a vacancy for every gadabout.
The grandest lodge awaits you—it won't sell out.

Ragged shore rocks nibble the soles of my feet,
as I wade in my slippery, rippling suite,
and draw the billowing curtains around me.
Maids change my sheets each split second for free.

Grand Marais resides at a spot in the galaxy
where lake witches waft to authenticate fantasy.
If you smell 'em, you'll see 'em, and bunk in the bay.
Marais enraptures at night, then rests radiant by day.

SPLIT ROCK LIGHTHOUSE
(Lake Superior)

On his tower windows, ice dangled like cleavers.
The gale erupted, in regal raiment of sleet.
He shivered in furs, woven from beavers.
A storm's cold cannonade thundered a drumbeat.
One freighter floundered on Superior's burial sheet.

His lighthouse whirled a dazzling fusillade,
a lantern dancing, prancing, pulsing, a guide
blazing a warning, a prophetic lightning rod,
foretelling hidden rocks below the boisterous tide
that skulk as scoundrels plotting homicide.

High upon a ragged cliff, the lighthouse keeper
hurled a circling spark above the savage lake.
Flashings flew above rapacious waves. Yet deeper
floats the moon above. She beheld his courage quake
and grinned at feeble beams below, winking to forsake

the freighter's fate. The keeper's brightening blink
paused between its flashes in the salvo of the snow.
Moonlight clutched the clouds to spy the freighter sink
and dwell as royal refugee in an undulating bungalow,
as Superior's haggard cargo and perpetual bedfellow.

The foghorn pounced upon the ship, as hammer on a nail,
and jabs of burning brightness leapt upon its reeling keel.
Shots of light and deathly wail then hailed a last travail.
Wild waves surrounded her to pound her welded steel.
What maniacal old mariner clutched the captain's wheel!

The freighter surged toward the rocks submerged ahead,
as do moths, unsought, untaught, advance upon a flame.
When blazes beckon, tread to cozy hearths, instead!
Let the radiant and rackety repel us with their fame.
Heed the keeper's warning, his summons for the dead.

MINNESOTA'S TEN MILLENNIAL GIRL

A Highway 59 repair crew found her,
near Pelican Rapids, nine feet below
yellow clay. Her skeleton lay without decay.

Beautiful bones survived ten thousand years.
When this proto-Indian lived, she knew her age,
just as I know mine—about midway to come what may.

She resurrects a glimpse of history,
the mystery now nearer to our touch.
She cracks creation and unpacks serenity.

Our minds grip her, against her will, to snatch
antiquity, as though we've unearthed a divinity
who waves her wand, and we abscond beyond

the borders, the barriers, the ticks and tocks.
When clocks stop, something better begins.
Her bones own freedom. We rate its features.

She seizes prestige. She's a legend
who parks on our planet but perches in passions.
Her shell brushes rarified air. She's somewhere

in both places, in a dazzling wasteland,
sprung as an artist awakening our wishes.
Maybe, in ten thousand years, my remains

will surface to astound a dumbfounded gardener.
"A find! One of a kind!" she will say of me.
But she'll never know my mind.

BLUE MOUNDS STATE PARK

Morning mists shroud iron-red cliffs.
Before sunset, the sky crouches,
bathing the reclusive mounds blue.

In a land of lakes, this prairie sprawls, strewn
with boulders, as though glaciers seeded pebbles
in the Indiangrass, planting a garden of stones,

now overgrown with an assortment of rock families.
Cliffs rose from below. Stones rained from above.
Long ago, hostility seethed between quartzite and ice,

followed by quarrels between other transient tribes,
more principled spats, hardheaded dissents
about possession of land, a day's worth of dominion.

A haze creeps. Its camouflage erases
the mounds. Hear the war whoops
of yesterdays. Hear the grass sway.

Fenced in, a bison herd putters, like indigent actors
re-creating their roles in sagas of ancient stampedes,
and so do we, who grandstand in our quiet corral.

The rubble of rocks squats, scouting the hereafter,
foretelling the next battle, divining the sequel.
In time, rampages shrink. Wee wars make you think.

WINONA BREW

At Winona, the Mississippi River looks back,
pondering the distinctions of liquid and land.
An island society huddles, mutineers in the water.

The river dodges its duty to discover Dubuque.
Rivulets gallivant, hedging allegiance,
demurring fealty to gravity's sagacity.

Pedestrian bridges sprout atop every lazy lagoon,
as pedestals for snow, as shade for the ether below.
By April, footprints on the bridge walk on water.

When a river ruptures and weaves waves
through miscellaneous channels and manifold veins,
some of its genial ambivalence spills ashore.

A dozen breweries and brew pubs moor
in Winona, Minnesota. Each mug I've hoisted
evinces the capricious crisscross of the river.

A skeptic, a maverick, a cavalier raconteur,
an eccentric dissenter, this gadabout river
exposes mercurial viewpoints that vault to the malt

and hop upon hops, till each pint possesses
the conundrum of creation and the riddle
of that aquatic kingdom flooding our wits.

Dip your stein in the big river for your aperitif.
Then, in a Winona pub, count the rings on your mug,
abridging the miles between splasher and splashed.

PAULETTE BUNYAN

With one boot anchored in Brainerd
and one boot barging Bemidji,
Paulette Bunyan arced her axe
to raze Akeley's forests
of Norway pine. A lumberjack
legend and behemoth logger,
Paulette could slash every grove
with one sweep of her blade,
and thunder leapt out before lightning
could put on its pants. Whirlwinds

erupted when her backswing rebounded.
Paulette drank a lake for a thirst quencher
in sunny July when waters twinkle
and broadcast the blue of the sky.
Paulette ate only dinosaur eggs,
she'd unearthed when her hatchet
split the subterranean turf. Paulette
filled her pipe with sawdust and twigs,
and her puffs of white smoke created
all the clouds existing today, so they say.

Paulette never knew one woodsman at all,
and, far as we know, no man wandered
the northland back then. Maybe men never

existed at all until Paulette pulled her big blunder.
One lone monster pine, eight thousand feet tall
and a few hundred around, challenged Paulette
to a showdown: "You ain't enough 'jack,
and you ain't got enough axe to topple
my towering column. Bestow your best swing.
I'll stand here for eons after your ending."

Paulette spit a wad of saliva and launched a new lake,
and she shaved a fine edge on her blade by chewing
the metal till her cudgel bore a razor-rimmed cleaver.
Paulette gripped her mallet, sharp as a switchblade,
in two gargantuan hands, and tilted the axe before
the brutal attack. Her whirling swing cut a whistling
crescent through the thunderstruck air and carved
the big pine down its diameter from crown to roots.
But then, in a flash, a phantom flew out.

The first Northwoods man sprang to life
from the heartwood of the tree.
Call him Paul Bunyan, a bona fide brute,
and no tree at all, except for the bark.
Paul and Paulette quarreled like territorial
beasts, though at least not as bad
as husbands and wives. Paulette finally
drifted to a Canadian province, where
legends are narrated in French.
Paul's agent insisted he borrow
Paulette's best exploits and take
his act to the Twin Cities.

DINKYTOWN USED BOOK STORE

Rain pounced upon Fourth Street,
drenching my daily agenda,
soaking my socks within seconds.

A sane asylum, the bookstore
beckoned, a port in my storm,
an oasis past a collegial door,

and I barged into the bowels
of the secondhand bookshop,
as though I'd implanted a brain

in the skull of the creature,
embedding my wits within
the backbone of stacked books,

the bric-a-brac chimneys,
the rectangular masonry,
the boxed paper layers

of peelable skins, teeming
with text, rotund from upholstery
caged between cardboard.

There, in one narrow alley,
shrouded, as though lost
in the raiment of rain,

an opus on exploits,
a tome on thinkable things,
a story of cloaked episodes,

a tale tattling the quests
of a fantasist, a facsimile of me,
caroled its summons to ascend

to the store rafters, whereabouts
my legend lodged, as a monk,
awaiting my inevitable advent.

A stepladder leaned on the edges
of ledges of lofty bookshelves.
I scaled rungs stacked like scrolls,

rolled centuries ago, a skeletal
keyboard, an orchestra spotlighting
the percussion department.

Climbing the ladder, I sought
one timeworn book that summoned me
to our rendezvous high overhead.

Innumerable footfalls raised me
to the pinnacle of a book galaxy,
whereupon a parcel of pages,

a bundle of sheets, a manuscript,
a yellowing cellulose, a stained
lignin husk, fluttered its feathers.

I pored over my story, flipping
the leaves of the saga, part
allegory, part potboiling pulp.

Then, my adventure suspended
at page 264. Someone absconded
with 265. I'm missing a paper.

As evinced by notes in the margins,
other readers had wrestled this book,
maybe the last chapters too.

What hijinks ensued in this missing scene,
maybe a scandal, or frivolous fame,
or a fortuitous gain we all crave?

Another bookworm had nibbled my myth,
maybe swallowed its pith, or looted
the hour of time the page carted.

In all candor, I've pilfered a few pages
from dusty bookshops, myself, not
to steal, rather, to heal the spine

of the spiel. To this day, I wonder
whether I'd butchered your books,
carving your wounds after cursory looks.

ITASCA: MISSISSIPPI RIVER HEADWATERS

Beginning with a bashful blush,
she wandered north to tour the hush
near tamaracks, cattails, and sedge,
then thought to probe the eastern edge,
but soon reversed her blueprint's pledge,

zigzagging back, meandering south,
still twenty hundred miles until her mouth
arrives, where the Mississippi River rolls.
She'd sketched a question mark on ancient scrolls.
Ambivalence arose, chaperoning wavy strolls.

A river's birth alights like gentle twilight snow
upon a placid lake land, pristine forests know.
A leaking lakeshore overflows to pioneer
the mighty rampage rising, faraway from here.
A dribble daintily absconds to engineer

the waterway bisecting west from east.
A wading pond begat a surging beast
when infant rivulets arose, serene,
to irrigate each evergreen,
who gulped from her disgorged canteen.

Then drips brought forth a juggernaut,
the majesty all rivers sought.
Inceptions dawn. Deception rises,
in affably benign disguises
that floated faith but spill surprises.

MANKATO MAN
AND NATURE'S PLAN

A mythical Mankato man,
a legend, a garrulous old ghost,
proposed to jumble Nature's plan,
a bold, insulting boast.

Said he, "When Nature orders me to shake,
I'll pirouette instead.
When Nature leads me by a lake,
I'll dream of baking bread.

"When Nature's call coerces me
to follow tracks foreseen,
I'll flout her map. I'll climb a tree,
or something in between.

"If Nature rains upon my day,
I'll picnic anyway, and ask
for snow to crown my hideaway.
I'll portray a snowman, cloak, and mask.

"If landslides roll, if rivers flood,
if a hurricane attacks,
I'll frisk and frolic in the mud.
My backbone never cracks.

"Let lightning fuse my vertebrae.
I'll laugh at every flash.
After earthquakes, I still feel okay.
It's Earth who felt the crash.

"Let Nature honor gravity
as master of the deep.
I'll flaunt my grand depravity.
Each cavity, I'll leap.

"Electromagnetic bullyboys
can't boss a bloke like me.
Atomic force affords my tinker toys,
which I now rule facetiously.

"Though Nature penned a private plan
to supervise my life,
I contravene, because I can,
not just to garner strife.

"When Nature thought she'd licked me
and laid me in a grave,
She overlooked my trickery.
We phantoms misbehave."

MINNESOTA'S AWKWATOK

Though none hung a painted portrait
or photographed its features, wait
until the hour of creatures. Fate
abuses those who speculate
on beasts, at least, their feast.

The terror traipsing timberland
from Ely down to Holyoke
appears as mist, a jolly smoke
that manifests a crawling cloak
of fear, too near to here.

Some say the brute arose from trees,
a wanton spawn of Norway pine,
half wood, half man, the borderline.
No windows wink, no doorways shine
to sit, alit with it.

Denounce these falsifiers' claims!
This monster reified from lakes,
by manifesting snowfall's flakes,
when water's wonder undertakes
real life, the zeal, the strife.

In lakes, confront the Awkwatok,
the dents atop each liquid lid.

In forests, greet the northland's id,
the ghost in greenwood's pyramid,
hid amid its grid.

The Awkwatok exemplifies
the imp in Minnesota's wild,
the Sioux and Chippewa godchild,
the voyageur, bewitched, beguiled.
Unstitch a myth to find its niche.

You never met an Awkwatok?
You've never tasted freedom's feast!
When birds flew west, though eggs stayed east,
their freest feathers leapt, at least,
the Awk, the Wat, the Tok.

It nibbles at your fishing line.
It tugs upon the shiny bait.
It's never early, never late,
to absolutely decimate
fond hopes, old oaths, your horoscope.

But the Awkwatok reciprocates,
by hitching fish upon your hook.
Before your bait and tackle shook,
it fooled each fish to overlook
your amateurish, furnished lure.

The Awkwatok still roams the state,
at times, to aid, at times, to tease,

while murmuring like bumblebees
or aspen trees in the autumn breeze.
Beasts never stalk an Awkwatok.

MOSQUITOES AND LOONS

Two mystic birds. Two enigmatical hymns.
Near Brainerd's Gull Lake, their harmony swims

above waters, among the whispering pines.
Hear eerie wailing. Hear the hectoring whines.

In three mournful syllables, a lamentation
interweaves with a singular buzzing sensation,

a vibration akin to a kazoo or high-voltage cable.
One songstress hoots. The other sizzles, when able.

Haunting yodels spring forth from the alto of the duo
to censure its partner's screeching soprano.

A melody awakening rapture's disguise
alights from the one with the fiery red eyes,

the spiritual sprite of the lake. Angelic wings
ferry caroling through eternal winters and springs.

Upon this night, this anthem, this staunch serenade
sprang in ancient recital, in moonlight's masquerade.

When the one with the buzz silenced its wings,
I forbore its sting. When feasting, it no longer sings,

drinking its own weight of my blood, just a wee part,
while the archangel narrated the hymn of my heart.

RED RIVER FLOOD
(East Grand Forks, MN)

Bob up, blow in, or lie down.
Choose only one scourge when you storm our town.

If water poured itself as just one thing,
we'd know the shape of the heartaches you bring.

But the skies beget snows beget ice,
and Red River folks got to plan thrice.

A battalion of blizzards abandoned our Heaven
in the winter of nineteen hundred, ninety-seven.

Snow piles reached past every porch top,
where whirling white flakes sought to stop.

Frosty glaze congealed on the Red River roof,
and the stalled stream loitered, complacent, aloof.

The Red River flows north. Any carpet of snow
melts south to north, provoking the Red River flow.

A blockade of upriver ice will roll out its ravage,
spilling floods on the banks as a cascading savage.

Surrounding terrain spreads flat as a nail head.
This lush land arose from a primeval lakebed.

Around here, water can't figure what garments to wear.
March slept in rigid wraps. Then she goes bare.

In quick, quarreling winds, a swift April thaw
transfigured the town, releasing the river's outlaw,

catapulting across miles of houses, half buried
in brown slush, in everything its rush carried.

Despite heaping our sandbags high on the dikes,
no barrier holds when the Red River strikes.

Sirens screamed endlessly. Soldiers appeared,
some in big trucks, some in boats, and we feared

we'd not see our houses again after the evacuation.
When smoke arose downtown, I knew the duration

of unscheduled vacations extended until kingdom come.
The bridges flooded. We heard the warning bells drum,

then the electricity failed. Tap water started to stink.
Torrents drowned the town. Streets started to drink.

Horribly handsome—this lavish beast fathered a chaos.
The fire's fiery reflections kindled feverish pathos.

When everyone deserted the town, I fled to the attic
and lay about, listening to transistor radio static.

I hung a white flag on my porch, a sign I've departed.
In lighthearted ease, I believed I'd outsmarted

the Red River and an entire East Grand Forks town.
They say none died in this flood, except for the clown,

who went missing in action and never was found,
though a tale bobs around that he fled underground.

I fancied I'd copy fickle water's mercurial mien,
maybe gas, maybe ice, maybe stream, unforeseen.

THE TIMBER HOUND

That eerie eve, the hound drew near to wail,
quite near him now, as though upon the trail
of wretched quarry—palatable prey.
The quiet woods housed meager game to slay.
Perhaps this beast may lend its snout to scout
where venison and rabbit meat hide out.

Behind his flashlight's snooping streak, he cleaved
the ghastly black, alit, so he believed,
sufficiently in swathes of clarity.
At night, all souls beseech light's charity.
He stalked into the woods, to grasp, to gain,
enlightenment, where sylvan riddles reign,

where darkness magnifies, accentuates,
and contemplates its Stygian estates.
The hound preceded him, or else, the howl
arose from oaks and pines. Each vicious vowel
approached, advanced, encroached, ungodly grim.
Malevolency's march encircled him.

Among the pantheon of pines, these nests,
whose pillars cage its careless guests,
two hunters hunted victuals, a feast,
to mollify a man or sate a beast.

His flashlight failed. His heart refused to beat.
Two sought, one brought, a meal of meager meat.

LITCHFIELD, MINNESOTA BAKERY

Sprung from the slumbering night,
the baker follows the flashlight's halo,
its glowing hole, to her flour factory,

where harvests of grindable grains resurrect.
Alchemist, sorceress, the baker awakens
the power of flour to pamper a man.

Jubilant doughnuts float in oil, brought
to a boil. As the happiest hoops in creation,
all doughnuts labor in pregnancy

until they deliver a hole. The whole
of a doughnut rolls in a perpetual ring.
Bite anywhere there, but the whole

shrinks as the hole unrolls
till the hole's all that's left
in the grip of your fingers.

Flour and yeast ascend as a beast.
Add sugar and milk of a similar ilk.
Butter and eggs float the nutmeg.

Then sunrise's customers trickle
into the baker's gastronomical lab,
and fellowship flowers. Baker

and buyers inhale the paradisial air,
and an oath of intimacy sizzles
among this benevolent band.

Patrons sit, ringing and wreathing
a round table, devouring delights,
encircling the inscrutable hole
segregating each soul.

GRAND MOUND IN KOOCHICHING COUNTY

By the banks of Rainy River,
Grand Mound graves
exalt forbears,
elevating bygone braves

above the water's surging shore,
celebrating centuries before

Rainy River rose to ferry
leisure boats
and idle men,
toting anything that floats.

Erecting sacred burial mounds,
tribes trapped yesteryears in timeless grounds.

Naked bones seem best imagined,
camouflaged,
and cloaked in clay,
screened from quandaries we've dodged.

If Time retraced its forward pace,
we'd acutely comprehend this place.

Ancient times conceal their telling,
out of sight,
obscured, discreet,
underground or found at starry height.

As humps of history, these knolls
reach to us, and thus, unroll Time's scrolls.

SMALLTOWN BRAIN

No wonder wits no longer fit
behind your cranial bone.
You've stuffed your skull with city streets,
then traipse your lane alone,
the only path you'll own.

No brain begets an urban burg.
Each mind's a tiny town.
A smalltown village emanates
from underneath your crown,
like verbiage from a noun.

You live within the hamlet walls.
You're janitor. You're king.
You couldn't give directions, though,
to strangers, visiting
your psychosocial ring.

Encountering protagonists
who star in every play,
you've cast a stage of thespians
who do as dendrites say,
though axons lead astray.

No stoplights bother main street's rush.
No thought outranks the next.

One grocery store sells everything.
No shopper gets perplexed,
despite synaptic text.

While governing your village square,
as mayor—reelected, too,
you've minimized the township's crime.
The only thief is you.
The cops are you-know-who.

Your town boasts ample parking space
for stationing your dreams.
Museums flourish. Antique shops
still catalog your schemes,
abstractly, so it seems.

All fail at fitting smalltown brains
in megacity places.
Municipalities arise
devoid of mental faces,
bereft of brain's vast spaces.

BIG BLACK BEAR STATUE (NORTHOME, MN)

An eerie vapor hovered low atop dark Bartlett Lake,
at twilight, nettling nerves, now frightfully awake

in Northome, home to bygone's monumental tales.
I feared a rumor might bear true, and I sought trails

in pavements, far from howls of wolves, farther still
from habitation housing bears, whose visits will

molest my slumber. Tiny Northome looms in majesty,
a lord, the middlemost reality of Minnesota's diary.

Imagine Northome. She bestows a funnel's neck, a vent
that vacates streams of yesteryears, a flowing sent

to scrolls in history. North to south, west to east,
enormous entities accost her landscape. Not a beast,

but lakes and forests, also tribal reservations,
all mount as behemoths in terra firma stations.

At Northome, nature coalesced into a magic midway.
On this frosty night, wild breezes warned my stay

would prove erratically arranged. I risked a stroll
past lodges. Wilder whispers woke. Time's whole

antiquity dove down the town's fantastic funnel.
The past leapt onward, racing through the tunnel.

In grasping gravity, I beheld galactic tumbling,
the stars abruptly plunging, crashing—crumbling

the cosmos. Bartlett Lake now brushed my shoes.
Its lapping liquid warned that anarchy ensues

when tourists brave tame Northome late at night.
My dangerous finale rose to prove this water right.

Ahead, a bear, an effigy, a black statue, stood erect,
surveying a vacant sky, savage kingpin of his sect,

upon his hind legs, mimicking a sentry. Then I knew
'twas he who funneled yesteryears' spilled stew.

Upright he stood, as if he's fashioned out of wood.
But *he* poured out *our* past. Think a black bear could?

The beast yet roosts in Northome, bigger than a whale.
I can't return. He'll eat you, if you ever share this tale.

FRAZEE TO OLIVIA: THE BOUNDLESS BIG

During renovations, Big Tom, the world's largest
turkey statue, got accidentally incinerated.
Frazee, Minnesota, built a replacement turkey,
bigger and better, from steel and fiberglass.
The freed spirit of the first Big Tom waddled
160 miles south to Olivia, home of the biggest
ear of corn statue, a half-husked cob, two dozen
feet high, just like Big Tom. Tom enjoyed
the biggest corn-on-the-cob feast in history.

Pretty soon, all the biggest roadside attractions
wandered from their towns, in search of greater
notoriety. Pelican Pete from Pelican Rapids trekked
to Baudette, Garrison, Rush City, and Isle to gobble
up the biggest walleye statues in the world.
Then Pete swallowed, whole, the big but lifeless
tiger muskie at Nevis, the lutefisk in Madison,
the trout in Preston, the Erskine northern pike,
and a 65-foot muskie in Bena.

The giant boot in Red Wing hopped to Darwin,
home of the largest ball of twine, to get laced.
The Rothsay world's largest prairie chicken strolled
to Vergas and Virginia, Minnesota, homes of the

state's biggest loons. Pretty soon, the world's
largest mallard, in Wheaton, flew into the gathering,
despite its 20-foot mass of concrete and steel.
Ever notice that the Big want to keep company
with the Big?

But the Big always fail, whether empires
or dinosaurs. Only the tiny survive, the smaller,
the better. Fantasies fly big, bigger than cosmos,
though life subsists smaller than the most sensitive
signals of our senses. Tourists viewing the big birds
and gargantuan fish seek something aggrandized,
so unreal it seems real, a pause on the way
to somewhere, not the final destination.

The novel architecture vacillates, remodels, wavers,
as a different creation contrived in each mind.
The tourist, himself, fathers the desired dimensions.
One mysterious grin shrinks him to a galaxy's girth.

THE VOYAGEURS ON PIGEON RIVER

In 1700, short, bearded, buckskin-bedecked brawlers
squeezed into birchbark canoes and paddled,
before sunrise and after sunset, on Pigeon River,
the rippling border between Minnesota and Ontario.

Boundaries flow, redrawn and confirmed
each moment, by the watery wand of nature.
Strong as mules and poor as prisoners,
the French-Canadian voyageurs served

as the fur company's navy, transporting pelts
to the urban markets. Dakota and Ojibwe tribes
toiled as trappers of beavers, fox, bears, otters,
muskrats, and lynx. Bartering flourished. Tribes

acquired iron tools, brass kettles, guns,
woven cloth, and liquor. Swathed in sashes,
topped in feather caps, the Canadian bruisers
chanted French chorales as they rowed,

in defiance of the arduous journey,
and, as well, in carousal with the dazzling
domain they dissected. History's toughest
men reveled in the wildest wonderland.

High Falls on the Pigeon River pours
water down one hundred and twenty feet.
In pairs, the men lugged their canoes
and supplies through the shore's woodlands,

planning to return from their portage
back to the Pigeon on calmer
waters. Staccato raindrops drummed
on the canoe, now a canopy above

their heads, each tiny trickle
tracing the border between
the encroaching avenues of doom
and an ambient aura of salvation.

NEW YORK MILLS RAIN

This town splashes.
Water pirouettes here.
This place gets rinsed every hour
in invisible, freshening rain.
Tour the boat factory,
a technological toy land,
inventing lake chariots.
These folks stand uncannily
above the glacial glitter below.

Thank the Finns who toted
their zeal to the timber mills.
Visit a dozen neighborhood saunas.
Hurl rain upon sizzling rocks.
Feel the dry fry, as your skin
dribbles water, spilling the ills
you garnered that day.
Finnish flags exalt the wintery white
of the northland, the liquid sky blue
of nature's wild fluids. The Nordic Cross
rejoices in Christianity's crown.

The town roosts on the Continental Divide,
pouring its blessed cellar water
serendipitously to Manitoba and Texas.

But the town hoards the holiest pools
of sparkling sprinkles in a brew pub
on Main Avenue. I sat as a stranger,
balancing my butt on a barstool,
as a minnow among walleyes. I drank
Imperial Stout, and everyone smiled
their greetings. My baptism humanized me.

LAKE BEMIDJI GOOSE

The statues of Paul Bunyan
and Babe the Blue Ox
in Bemidji are aspirations,
neither as big as your dreams,
nor as polished and fussy as sculptures.
That's not the point.
Their theater stirs in your mind.
They offer a blueprint,
and you fill in the rest.

A lone goose floated on Lake Bemidji.
I hurled flakes of popcorn into the water,
and the white wafers rolled toward the goose
on shore waves, gently bouncing,
looking like a slow-motion gallop.
The goose snatched one puffed corn
and dragged it under the water,
shaking it, in a frenzy, to remove
the butter and salt.
Then her beak pulsed like a sewing machine
as she chewed and swallowed,
before stabbing the next miniature cloud.
Good things get coated with glaze.
Wash them off.

PART III:
inner outposts

PRIVATE PONDS

Our wits befit a sea's vast realm,
surrounding fond frontiers,
the galaxies that overwhelm—
as dolls, by puppeteers.

To dive into a briny deep
affrights intelligence,
as charcoal does a chimneysweep,
as pound notes do a pence.

Sole sailors glide on whisking waves,
in want of coastal surf.
No beach restrains our brains' enclaves,
devoid of shoreline turf.

A cosmos summons escapades,
in waterways unknown,
to hurl cerebral cannonades,
elation's chaperone.

A synapse sparks, excites, cajoles,
as artistry began.
Minds sail in oceanic bowls.
Each neuron scans the plan.

Each mariner upon our quest
awaits what fate foredooms,
some venturous, some wariest,
estranged from wondrous wombs.

Our deaths bestow the remedies
for cowardice and dread.
We sail upon uncanny seas,
cold quilts above the dead.

To drown in storms' adversities
seems little risk at all.
I'll swim among perplexities
and dive as a cannonball.

I'll plunge into the baffling brine,
where friends and fools reside,
where lush conundrums intertwine
my prize, personified.

Yet gaze upon society.
Few sailors brave the seas.
They seek ascribed propriety.
They seek grand guarantees.

Landlubbers gaze into a swamp
and wade a bit within
the puddle's shore, deprived of pomp,
till dire doubts begin.

On shore, they tap a tiny box
until a glimmer bonds
their plights to bytes, as laughingstocks,
aglow in private ponds.

SECRET SNOW BONES

I seek to sprout, inside out.
What you see—'tain't me. It parodies
the tawdry turf atop my true identity.
To know a man, ignore his surface bulletin.
Apprize the bones he owns. Scrutinize his skeleton.

Alabaster bones evince the mien of me,
the ivory wish, the pearly urge,
the snowcapped white benignity.
My principles shine as porcelain.
My scruples catapult like saintly salt.

Appraise the twinkles on my skullcap.
My ribs will gallivant in glitter.
My femur's flash could ruin a retina.
When my phalanges flare, they'll singe your hair.
Those secret snow bones—'tis me.

Just so, God resolves to manifest
His blueprint, His master plan for Man
in gentler terms than Noah's flood,
whenever frosty powders plunge from Heaven
to here, below, and topsoil's wrapped in snow.

Heaven's softest savages
float as frozen flakes

and drift as lodgers lent from nowhere.
Silent snowfall sows the land
with lost voyagers from celestial seas.

Like sheep's shorn fleece upon the fields,
snow convenes a gardenful of privacy.
Old barns and trucks collect new faces,
unwrinkled, stylish, young, and clean,
tiled with modern manna's loaf of charity.

Telephone wires ferry, one by one,
a flock of migratory mountain goats.
Jagged rooftops look rotund atop the splatter,
as though blanketed with pancake batter.
All points prove pointless now. Realities rise round.

Cold and white, ephemeral ghosts
foster fresh facades upon their hosts.
Yet could it be this snowy crust portends
the soul of earthly kin, while turf below
bestows its husk, nothing but its skin?

Contemplate this Artist's ingenuity,
deflating clouds to lay a quilt
upon humanity in hibernation,
silencing the bedlam, tranquilizing rage,
casting bygones under winter's cold new page.

Heaven's harvests sow the seeds of piety,
a whiteness as frigid as the Holy Writ,

a luminosity as brilliant as my bones.
Then the blessed blanket fades away,
and we gadabout, no longer inside out.

LAST LOVE

She dwells as a ghost story penned
upon my wit's writ, as a parchment
imprinted in penitence,
an apparition waylaying
the ledger of life in my lanes
of youthful pursuits, where one gains
the bounty of wages that wiles attain.

At twenty, her cannonade burst
upon indelicate desires
of mine to erase the chalked slate
cartooning my juvenile state.
Youth's loneliness rendered me ripe
for plucking my covetous stalk.
She'd detonate as my first love.

She'd evanesce as my last love.
Forever her memory prowls
as matron in hauntable halls,
traversing remembrance's maze,
attacking my tactics to shake
her edicts proclaiming the clout
of feminine fire to unwire

the prudence that safeguards a man
on his ladder's rational rungs.
What sorcery launched to enchant
a desolate hermit's desires?
Mysterious glamor allured
the fly to a spider's backroom
enwrapped in a rapturous doom.

'Twas she who enkindled my wick.
'Twas she whose invasive cascade
revived withered remnants of joy—
for a boy, near empty, now filled.
Then wretchedness reigned as a wraith.
She rose as a jurist and judge.
Each figment I fancied proved wrong.

Moreover, she latched on as a leech,
an anchor to drag me to depths
of the deep. I foresaw in her gaze
my wreckage, a ravaging raze,
erasing the rest of my days.
She straightened the curls in her hair,
perhaps as a gesture to me,

understanding we two grew aware
that we'd perched on a paramour's ledge,
but plunged irrevocably over the edge.
She vanished next day, so I thought,
but memory's caskets and urns

erupt in a froth to pervade
the haze of my mental arcade.

In gazes she granted to me
on her decisive departure, I marked
my shrinking induced her to think
upon a man's mettle, his worth.
So, too, disillusion suffered its birth
in me, in my hour of regret.
I flamed into love till love quenched

the symptoms of love, its mystique.
Dismay yet accosts me today.
Appraising a woman's allure,
I stir, then know I'm forever unsure.
But the hound of my madness rebounds
to scorch me again, to torch my desire
in ashes on passion's cruel pyre.

Never trust any mademoiselle,
save one—she, who toasted your heart
at love's launch, right from the start.
Her hauntings grow dearer to me.
Her smoldering fire flashes in unquenchable ashes.
Her shadow carved my cognitive scar.
Bless you, dearest, wherever you are.

LAUGHTER

What is laughter? What knits its knotty ovation?
Who fathered the flock of this alien invasion?
What brain runaways flee in these risible sneezes?
Do our snickering steams create facetious breezes?
Laughter erupts, then disrupts, any somber occasion.

From stitches unstitched, laughter tips status quo.
No maxims emerge that giggles can't overthrow.
What edifice mounts that titters won't tumble?
Few blueprints sketch what jeering wouldn't jumble.
From a cranial hole, flurries of farce overflow.

Our craniums crack when the cackling springs.
Other skulls split to receive laughs a joke brings.
Uncannily, laughter launches a jocular jab
into intellects, keen to esteem laughter's stab.
Laughter jests best with stings from genial swings.

Sages say laughter flaunts our superiority.
They posit laughs leap to confront incongruity.
Laughs may accrue to calm violent storms.
Nervous puffs might signal the violation of norms.
Girls neigh at horseplay. Raillery squires sexuality.

One pastor, whom I know, proclaimed laughter arose
to conquer the quagmire of carnal imbroglios.

Laughter bestows our visceral pathway to prayer.
He chuckled these words. His gust pulsed in the air,
a draft that wafted my pastor's comical blows.

Every sinner and saint will laugh what he knows.

RENDEZVOUS

Raindrops march as sailors do,
sliding in an ocean's bowl,
flooding down a tombstone's hole.

Puddles float their childhood toys.
Tombstones top these navy boys.
Tandem squadrons rendezvous.

Names engraved in a granite wall
glisten when the raindrops fall,
marching memoirs none recall.

MACHINE CHUCKLES

I love to catch them grin at me
before each snicker hurls
a tittering, a mockery.
Their cackling mirth unfurls.

Machines are geared for levity.
They rattle out mean jokes.
They giggle at an obscenity,
until each rivet smokes.

Repairmen rouse more jolly rants,
guffaws, then raucous laughs.
An owner's groans ignite their chants
of giggling epitaphs.

Refrigerators chortle twice
as much as heaters howl.
A dead, defunct, deceased device?
Find comics on the prowl.

The widgets cluck and chuckle more
when motors bust a gut.
For sure, hilarity's in store
when factory doors are shut.

I fancy every machine
slaps cream pies in my face
and cackles like a wicked queen
burlesquing my disgrace.

But I'm the one still snickering.
They'll laugh until they die.
They lack the knack for bickering.
They lack the will to lie.

THE BELIEVABLE DISTANCE

If I stood an inch closer to you,
you'd see in my pupils, in my pores,
my insincerity. You'd feel it, smell it.
If I stood a foot farther away,
you'd detect my indifference.
I achieve relevance to you
when I stand at the Believable Distance.

Rethink the survival of the fittest.
Evolution advances from outliving
and outlasting your neighbors
by spotting the optimal orbit

between you and the turbulence, the rumpus,
the jeopardy that troubles your sanctuary,
threatens your refuge, assails your asylum.

From every danger point, you must determine
the optimum radius to shield you from the carnage,
but permit you the first scavenge of the scraps.

Our ancestors survived as split-second surveyors,
who scrutinized the gap, diagnosed the dimensions,
gauged the breadth, adjudicated the interval
between opportunity and annihilation.
You see it in yourself, even today.

You seek a reassuring remoteness in intimacy,
a sweet spot where the span affords you credibility.
The Believable Distance resides at only one spot,
specified in space-time coordinates.

Ancient forefathers laced their genes
with this innate aptitude.
Else, Mankind would molder and vanish.

Then the writers arrived.
The Believable Distance devolved.

ANCIENT APATHY

Earth's indifference hardens us, sharpens us.
Mother Nature knew we'd tussle. Tough or die.
Laud her lash, however dire her discipline.
We forbear, while weaklings wonder why.

Pain pounds. Good, fire tempers steel
and builds elastic, hardy, indefatigability.
Nests of nerves infest our frames, squealing,
solely there to howl, to shriek, to bellow constantly.

Think of it and you'll agree. If pain afforded peace,
we'd destroy ourselves in seeking torture's ecstasy.
Pain instructs us: lengthy living fosters agony.
Seek the gain of quietus, its deadly, dark serenity.

Find expiry's balm, its calm, unassuming truancy.
Ancients sang of mythic gods nurturing Man's affairs.
Petition Zeus and Jupiter to intercede in suffering.
No. For pain's our fame. Ask a God who cares.

TEETER-TOTTER

Teeterboards rock in pendulum swings.
One end arises, one end descends,
like precarious flights on a pelican's wings.
At opposite seats of the seesaw, two friends
or two foes, the two aspiring kings

balance, pivoting upon a linear lever,
perched on an axis, a fulcrum, a hinge,
the swivel, the spindle, the midmost achiever
of rhythmic rotations for two fools on the fringe.
Each rider bounces, but each remains a believer

that the next swivel, rotation, gyration, or spin
will finally go 'round the circle, complete a full turn,
the consummate pirouette, the paramount win,
justifying the journey, absolving a ceaseless sojourn,
more man now than mannikin. Flesh freshens your skin.

Just so, two titans tussle upon the seesaw of Time.
Remembrance plants its rump atop one swaying seat.
Possibility squats flabby cheeks in past's pantomime.
Both riders roll to compete without pushing their feet.
Possibility poses lyrics. *Remembrance* rattles rhyme.

As the linchpin, the keystone, the mainstay, and crux,
the mighty fulcrum, Time's axle, a wee cardinal point,

pivots the seesaw, slants its slope, fatefully plucks
from *Possibility*'s treasures, the jewel to anoint
Remembrance, bridging two realms, frothing in flux.

Bygone's maybes, past's perhaps, a shadow's perchance
abide at destiny's door, a lever's infinitesimal gate,
where serendipity will segue to breach and advance
Possibility's noise to *Remembrance*'s joys, then await
memory's capricious romance, lost in antiquity's trance.

BATHED BRAIN

All the rain in my brain splashed to mystify
my inquisitive scrutiny
of reality, truth, and the certainty
that my wits sit afloat, nearly dry.

If the drizzle descends to my own cellar floor,
will my brain hide in the attic, remaining ashore?

During downpouring days in my psyche's sole suite,
a thunderstorm rose,
around Gray, across White, like a swung garden hose,
flooding my closets of cranial meat.

Cerebellum, cerebrum, and frontal lobe,
in a cannonball dive, disrobe,

and embark on a snorkel to otherwhere,
where all maritime minds submerge,
where plummeting sky and the formerly dry converge.
Before bathing, wait, rate the humidified air

in each precinct, in each plot dethroned,
in each noble quest postponed.

As I waited and waited for the rain to cease,
all the raindrops dressed in snow,

in their wintery wraps, in their bungalow,
in the realm of refugees.

Then the frost in the flurries confessed its death
as the breeze unmasked its breath.

LUMBERING BRAIN

If brains arose from lumberyards,
my mind gets simplified.
Electric wiring's labyrinth?
Foresee a playground slide!

Each nerve begets a two-by-four,
each synapse deemed a nail.
We'll reacquaint from carpentry.
We're hammered head-to-tail.

While axons ache to tingle-talk,
my woodwork murmurs, mild,
esteemed as queen of quietude,
aroused, but never wild.

Though dendrites dangle, temptingly,
to catch an axon's pitch,
my hardwood scaffold beats a brain,
in scratching any itch.

Feel free to sear a tattooed face
upon my timber arm.
My wooden nerves will never mind.
My heart's exempt from harm.

If hinges hook my haunches' edge,
adore me now—a door.
I'll swing to scenes on either side,
a portal, evermore.

While nerves get sheathed in cozy robes,
as plush as bunny tails,
my lumber flaps like baseball bats,
as tough as killer whales.

Though nerves might feel profusely smote,
the ecstasy subsides.
Enlist a tree's stability.
Be wood, be good, besides.

BRAIN RIVER

I rowed on rivers in my mind,
upstream of cataracts,
but paddling wrought futility.
I oared against the facts.

Downstream portends of waterfalls,
beyond my fountainhead.
I pulled against the current's flow,
one stroke ahead of dead.

GUARD DOG

I chained my brainstem's hungry beast
atop my spinal cord.
Escaping, starved for self-esteem,
the ego's overlord,

it vandalized my frontal lobe,
inciting Matters Gray.
With narcissism's harpsichord,
the beast began to play.

LAYERS

Vibrating, colliding, my atoms got hot,
but not hot enough. I wore layers
of garments inside my winter parka.
I sought nirvana, that immaculate spot
where my heat found nowhere to go,
and the cosmos agreed it didn't need me,
anymore, to sustain thermal equilibrium.
Snowflakes descended, not as slow rain,
but as minnows swimming the air,
meandering down, in due time, but first climbing

back up an invisible staircase, only to tumble
again. Not lost or astray, they know the way.
Someone gives them a nudge. This choreography
appears an improvisation, but an old scroll scripted
each prance in the dance. Then at intermission,
the theater turned black. I slept till the second act.
The new scenery stacked snow hats on the trees.
It looked like trees sprang up from under the carpet
of snow, wearing a white cap but no shawl.
But bare patches of grass betrayed the playwright's

illusion, where a broom swept the white confetti away.
Amazingly, I've never complained before.
From the story's foreshadowing, I anticipate

that the script casts me in some bit part
in the third act, but I'll get typecast again
as the old guy in layers. Then the playwright
flatters me, saying, "You *own* this part." It's crazy,
but this galaxy maintains, gainfully employed,
every graviton, photon, orbit, and force field.
Someday I'll quit, but I'll never get fired.

SUNLIGHT STOOPED

Sunlight stooped to read my opened page,
creeping stealthily past paragraphs,
tickling ink spots, brightening the stage,
tinseling the chapter, stifling laughs.

Moonlight slyly snooped, forlornly drawn
down the book's penultimate adieu,
mirroring sunlight's prophesies of dawn,
yet evading vows the sunlight drew.

THE IMPERSONATOR

An amateur agreed to play my life,
if granted broad artistic license, taking
liberties, in an otherwise credible facsimile.

A third-rate actor, more a pantomimist,
he fancied he'd portray me, charitably,
and hence I overpaid him, handsomely.

Misunderstandings festered from the start.
I'd not engaged him to portray my past.
I'd assigned him as creator of my futurity.

Since I'd exhausted every conceivable blunder
in past misadventures, I sought professional help
to misjudge, fumble, stumble, flub, and botch

my remaining days in bold, inventive episodes,
not in prosaic failures, mundane miscues,
shopworn screwups, or stale miscalculations.

After some slight success, he knew he got me hooked
and extorted me for further payments. His skills
as a shakedown artist, surprisingly, revitalized me,

and soon I'd depleted my savings, voluntarily,
in anticipation he'd grow into the role of raising me
from a pedestrian imbecile to quintessential clown.

Then my scheme cracked, crashed, and cratered.
With money to burn, this actor subcontracted
another actor to play him, playing me. And you can

guess the rest. Seven further layers of impersonators
lounge around this town. They're kind of funny, sure,
but some of their escapades hit me in the pocketbook,

and today, seeking to satisfy my debt collectors, I
took a job impersonating a guy who masqueraded
as a guy tenfold removed from the guy portraying me.

I don't know why I seem to always get into these crazy
jams. Anyway, you now know it wasn't me who pulled
any hijinks not erased by the statute of limitations.

THE OUTSIDE

The outside tries to get inside me.
I close my curtain, making certain
no outreach of light might beseech
me to surrender. She seeks to send her
outdoor essence over to my presence.

Light intrudes, as a dubious aura, or a
wayward weight, making my space
seem heavier, when seen, unscreened
by the warmth of darkness. Swarms
of clarity, barely caring their carousing

incites me, invite me into unsightly light.
Recall that birds abjure from all stirrings
at night. After-hours, their mighty powers
wain, the way my slumber seeks to sunder
the wide wings of glowing, outside things.

SALT AND SNOW

A snowflake totes iniquity,
at heart. Debris festoons its core
and seeds the crystal's symmetry.
A grimy rogue, all ice deplore,
resides inside, upon the filthy floor.

The oceans carry secret salts,
obliviously everywhere,
as souls unbound within their vaults,
in nowhere, lost in liquid's thoroughfare,
perambulating paths of prayer.

Exposed to vapor, Heaven's breath,
the ghosts, invisible no more,
emerge as remnants after death.
Not hid nor hazy, as before,
the self awaits at rapture's door.

UNSTILL BIRTH

Abstractly borne in boats, the mind
will row upstream to shores behind.
Our wishes sail arrears, reversed,
to yesteryears, whose hours rehearsed
the script for what each dawn will find.

No sailors row their boats downstream,
where callous currents dash their dream,
unless their oars could flee the tombs,
returning them to cherished wombs,
the genesis of self-esteem.

Do blessed stillbirths celebrate
their hasty leap to Heaven's gate?
Grace snuffed their candles' feeble flames,
before misdeeds denounce their names.
Departing early, never late,

for blest festivities we seek,
cherubic children's exits speak
of peace. Beat back your vessel's oars.
Unstill birth awaits on bygone shores.
Life's delta dissipates life's creek.

WIND AND MUSIC

She wandered, a fugitive wind,
sprung from a runaway storm.
Her wind rustled some men,
brushing susceptible scalps,
then vanishing, leaving nothing
behind. The wind swept near them,
never unloading tangible tales.
Her wind ferried her fragrance,
an aroma of a desolate launch
from forlorn blustery precincts.

An ambiguous aura hovered,
then dispersed in her flight,
abandoning each fleeting milieu.
No one recalled her bewildering halo.
She flared as she fled.
Her presence lingered
for a discomfiting moment,
as an agitation in the ambience.
Then she forsook possession
of each notion she'd nudged.

Her wind advanced upon me,
as though my mind cradled
the haven her gust sought.

Her breeze toted a music.
Beakers of song gorged
my brain. She meant her songs
to fill, then spill, trickling from me,
leaving me once again dry.
Her music sought silence,
but her anthem plays on.

FAILURE

Failure submerges like a sunset,
a flattening flare,
a delirium that dangles,
then capsizes,
hauling all of Heaven to Earth's cellar.
Then the indifference of night
brushes you, passes you by,
not acknowledging awareness of you.
Night unfurls stillness.
Sounds murmur, unheard.
Time pauses.
Expectations teeter and taunt.
You wish for the crash.
The inky silhouette of a tree
whispers something,
something important to you,
the hushed aspirations,
the fading fumes of the bygone.
You feel tranquil, placid, serene,
at repose. A gate opens.
You breach the border.
The burden of duty and liability vanishes.
Liberation elates you.
You've overcome role and rank.

The collapse of light exempts night
from requisite wardrobes, and the fabric
of your idle, ethereal entity drifts
through the easy night breeze,
ruffling the dawn of your denouement.

PART IV:
family and faith

MINNESOTA SAINTS

In more than twenty northern towns,
the saints contribute names.
Add Francis, Martin, Louis, Croix,
to Mary, Michael, James,

and Vincent, Rosa, Anthony,
to Bonifacius, Clair.
Augusta, Charles, and Joseph
dwell miles from Saint Hilaire.

When Leo barred Attila's Huns,
no northland village stood
upon the prairie near Spring Creek,
confessing Leo's sainthood.

A sobriquet, of course, Saint Cloud
renounced his royal gains,
to fix this monk's fidelity.
His legend's lore remains

in central Minnesota's plains.
Through snowstorms, all the saints
endure a wintery, wild realm,
without outward complaints.

May God bless French explorers' souls.
Their tours perpetuate
the faith transcending centuries.
They named. We emulate

the saints who rouse our virtue,
our desire, and our thirst
for exploring proxy places,
where saints adventured first.

Apostle Peter dwells in County Nicollet.
Tornados test the town.
Saint Peter might deny, at first,
but not when roofs crash down.

Saint Peter's citizens proclaim
allegiance to Christ's crown.
A dash of dear divinity
endows the town's renown.

Apostle Paul arrives each fall,
when autumn leaves descend,
reminding folks, Damascus dawns
at any highway's bend.

How many denizens rethink
upon persisting doubt,
when city signs announce their name,
and hope Saint Paul hops out!

The martyr, Stephen, now resides
as saint of County Stearns.
Forgiveness harbingered his fame,
as every toddler learns.

Thank God, we left towns' naming rights
to voyageurs, tribes, and preachers.
Imagine the noxious names we'd bear,
if bestowed by modern overreachers!

Our Minnesota saints inspire
triumphant blessedness.
A name's an aspiration. Find
an epithet's caress.

Tomorrow's saints await to hatch
from snowy shells up north.
Encounter one in Saint Hilaire,
just one the Lord sends forth.

THE PARENT'S HOUR

Before the sun inaugurates
each workday's enterprise,
the children, half asleep, surmise
maturity awaits,
beyond the morning's guarded gates.

Amid the clattering of dishes,
within the children's fictive castle tower,
arrives the Parent's Hour.
Their parents whisper secret wishes
until the kitchen faucet swishes.

What drowsy children hear
emerges cloudily,
as murmurs seeping randomly,
eliciting arousal, a furtive fear
dispatched to brush a pillow-muffled ear.

In beds' warm realms, reclusive refugees
envisage isolation,
a foreigner's sensation.
A groggy child attempts to grasp the mysteries.
But vagaries persist, too many to appease.

The father, armed with a toolbox, leaves,
alighting next in a factory's gloom.

The mother steps inside the children's room,
to ready them for school, and each receives
one slice of light that every dawn achieves.

FATHER AND SON

I.

To be a father's son grows bothersome,
past seventeen long years of royal reign,
when freedom's overture begins to drum
in boisterous burrows of teenage brain.
His impudence miscounts my monstrous cost,
in rank and rectitude. Once wild, now mild,
a middle-aged tomcat, now tamed, limps, lost
behind my child, jury-judged before trialed.
His gambols amble. My old figments leapt.
My trance transcends his irrational dreams,
as swept conflagrations. He cried. He crept.
A wee spark I hosted toasted my schemes.
Clouds crouched, caressing me, on his natal date,
when hoisting his incommodious weight.

II.

Today, the freeloader forsook our nest.
He's cheerful, fearful. He's discovering
his pilgrimage west, a college's guest,
beyond mothering, hyper hovering.
A dorm room mimics a jejune saloon,

a haven harboring collegial clowns,
devoid of lustrous sun, as rote as the moon.
For caps and gowns buy nepotistic crowns.
Find grins on my kid. Of me, he'll be rid.
One score minus three, he's forsaken me.
He recalls every deed I misdid.
Travails devoured past hours. Flashbacks come free.
Yet heartstrings revive in counterattack.
When I gazed beyond, he turned and looked back.

MOTHER AND SON

If mothers try personifying jailhouse guards,
we know the inmates get away with crimes.
All boys resist the tyranny of prison yards,
and mothers' sons comply in pantomimes.

Forgiven, coddled, fostered, nurtured, idolized,
and granted amnesty, each pampered son alights
as charming ignoramus, a German Shepherd prized
as family buffoon—his sins, mere oversights.

When I beguiled my wife into matrimony's chain,
our son arose in regal garments, celebrated, praised
by Mom for paltry deeds. She cheered his meager brain.
But Mom disparaged Dad, disintegrating, dazed,

who wondered where abandoned boyhood fled.
Though mothering acquittals purge his progeny
of criminality, recall this imp's trajectory will head
toward future fatherhood, apropos aforesaid infamy.

Wives forget that boyhood lasts and perseveres.
Though she seeks to fix your imbecilic shame,
demand confession of her hostility toward years:
"Alright, alright, I'll treat all juveniles the same."

MY PICTURE POSTCARD

Eternity mailed a picture postcard to me.
My paradisal precinct still beckons, it seems,
prancing upon its bright picture-side gleam,
flashing exotic, utopian scenes.

The artist's vast canvas swept extravagantly,
and so, I fancied, for certain, at least maybe,
this picture prevails, as well, perpetually,
upon the postcard's backside, dazzlingly.

But the flipside lay lifeless, as barren as Mars,
naught but the cardboard's aimless, rectangular face.
No scrawling, no script, no scribble, nor scars
graced the forlorn panorama's white space.

A smudge blemished the desolate upper-right edge,
where a postage stamp ought to squat as the host.
But surplus saliva leapt off its ledge,
abandoning its post, shedding its ghost.

No ink piloted this placard toward my address.
Yet a message whistled—just for me, for my rank—
and whispered out from its vacant crevasse,
out from the breadth of its bottomless blank,

whence we write and read our own sordid life story.
Though a postcard totes a pint-sized tabloid,
a kingdom's choir beckons—a glory
beyond barriers that varnish its void.

I scribed one Word on this tiny, ticketed square,
assuming I'd suffice as the sole recipient.
Undaunted, under His immaculate care,
I penned the portraiture of points that He'd meant.

One Word illuminated the labyrinth inside
as I spied my paradisal postcard revived.
Deity and deviant sought to collide.
I wrote one righteous Word. Pictures arrived.

WHAT'S THE CATCH?
(My Cat's Name)

'Tis my fame as a savior of wandering cats
that roused me to rescue these runaway brats.
A wee kitten beseechingly scratched at my door
before patiently licking the rags that she wore,

as though prettying up to await her new roost,
when my intertwined fingers bequeathed her a boost.
Not a glimmer of gratitude glowed on her face,
not a hint to acknowledge the granting of grace.

'Tis no more than all cats of distinction deserve.
Let we masters remonstrate, if we have the nerve.
Though my kitten is smitten with ruining my rug,
the awardee of her carnage delivers a hug.

Under furniture slashed lies a saucer of cream,
as though I'm the obsequious serf of our team.
All altruism garners her glare of disdain,
with raw rancor rebuking my menial brain.

On the notion that I'm a redeemer of cats,
wisdom pounced upon me after one of our chats.
With the savvy of saints in forswearing their fame,
my idea emerged—I'll decide on her name.

After blessings, what query yet rings in her mind?
With each mercy, what puzzle perplexes her kind?
Is she pondering how to explain this mismatch?
Doing good as a gift for my bad?—What's the catch?

Strolling the yard, "What's the Catch?" knows her name,
as she preens like a showgirl, evincing no shame.
"What's the Catch?" so said I, and let biddings invoke
my whimsical wit in our family joke.

'Twas a glorious morning in dazzling June,
in a season when nightingales tattle my tune.
But cascading from Heaven's domain, I then heard
a Voice roar out this moniker, word-upon-word.

What's the Catch? I knew the Voice called to us all.
Our blessings abound, but our gratitude's small.
In the thunder from Heaven, the halloos proclaim,
What's the Catch? to us freeloaders, taunted by name.

ELEGY FOR A NOBODY

Gazing at her open coffin, I clutched, within my fist,
a never-opened, sealed envelope, a secret elegy,
scripted by herself, a lamentation's howl of grief,
to be read by me, at her funereal finale. There
she slept in silk pajamas. A single fancy trinket
adorned her breast. One must wonder what words
she would compose to befit her last repose.

Shouldn't an elegy mine the ore of metaphors?
What curious requiem had she contrived, rehearsed,
and written for this day? Perhaps its author anguished
over every syllable of these chosen words, her treatise
tendered to resurrect sentience from the grave.
No culprit will accrue conclusive credit for her death.
We fancy her heartstrings' demise heralded her end.

Time plucks us all to the margins of engraved memories.
As she got sicker, we shunned her, as though
her mortality might spread as a ghastly contagion.
Her flirt with death might flash upon any bystanders,
exposing us as ripened and full-bloomed targets
for Death, that demon appalled by immortality,
a creature fond of ends. Though we sought no lessons

on how to die, perhaps her elegy sought to diagram,
from her blueprint, requisite steps, the fading,
inch by inch into the infinite. Her Godly faith
lingered, locally legendary. Her certitude of future
episodes bestowed the model for celestial sequels,
an aftermath devoid of statisticians. Her cozy clique,
in God's sorority, ruffled our aplomb. Perhaps as His

secretary, she inscribed, in her self-authored elegy,
the memoranda of sanctity. Her piety descended
as an affront to us. If God weighs in on her side,
He's not attending to us. We feared she gained
covert insight lacking in us, for her former voice
spoke of a cryptic connection to the otherworld,
a Christian cosmos that she knew too intimately.

Indeed, we feared that her entrance might complete
a paradisal realm's quota. Worst of all, she appeared
to hide her knowledge from us, as though her secret
would overwhelm our wits. Her simpleness seemed quaint.
So we scoffed: *It's she who's afraid to look foolish.*
Her death roused no tears, no drooping faces,
no cracked voices, no affectionate anecdotes. None

in her tiny funeral service wearied a handkerchief.
She'd lingered, expecting to die, a desert flower.
Yet we harbored a haunting that Death might return,
now that his long-drawn assignment found fruition.
For she'd seemed to preside as gatekeeper of Death,

and her absence foretold the storming of strongholds
we'd leased as lodgers on an outskirt of her fortress.

Her bemused smile conveyed insights appreciated
by none, for her gestures depreciated our serenity.
As amateur painter, her brush dabbed so few colors
beyond the dominant one. Perhaps she fancied
her simplicity bespeaks genius. But maybe we mistook
her intent. Won't every fool fancy a sunrise profound?
Unmarried introverts frighten everyone. We presume

they conceal something grave, grander than graves,
from critical eyes. Loners always forebode a surprise,
but her demure deference signaled something more.
She never saw herself as a topic worthy of discourse.
I've concluded she intended to menace our town,
provoking our interminable pondering upon the blow
we'd suffer when her dispatch sprang forth, uncovered.

I fancy we, the alive, those still standing, bequeath
the canopy casting her shade, and our absence might
illume this dazzling grandam evermore. Strewn across
her placid coffin, buoyant shadows crept, shade flung
by mortals, by the unborn, and by wisps of wickedness
subsisting before. No trophies or bugles will favor
her grave. Dates carved in her stone already fade.

We never thought of her as fully alive. Yet at this hour,
her phantom survives. Those two pages, birth, death,
a launch, a climax, misapply to her life. Inexplicably,

her antecedents and successors roam as her replicas.
Fancy what might have been! If she'd once hatched
a ribald joke, or she'd left a legacy of queer quotes,
or if her wardrobe ever hinted at gaudy or grace,

why, then, we could mark her as dead, as once alive.
But she clutches a furthermost secret that she drags
to her grave. Yet, had we but once beseeched her,
in life, to tell all, her face might hover among us,
detached from her soul. It was I who discovered
the script tucked under the Bible that lodged
on her deathbed's nightstand. I flinched. She!

She had composed her own elegy! Or so
the sealed edge of the folded paper proclaimed.
My trembling fingers clutched this thesis, as though
I reached through Death's veil. Yet I felt stunned
by her evinced indifference to poetic decorum.
'Tis for the living to write elegies.
'Tis for the dead to revive in versed visions.

At her open coffin, I'd struggled with doubts.
I dallied. I dithered. Should I open
her sealed post and reveal its avowals
to the sparse congregants there?
We fidgeted. We stalled till I tossed
the testament, the locked letter,
into her burial box before closing the lid.

A COVEY OF CRITIQUES

Women convene a secret society,
where they train girls from birth
to demean men constantly,
so men sputter and stall,
always on the defensive,
and won't find time to articulate
the cavernous faults of every woman.

Critical thinking requires objectivity,
a dispassionate analysis
that precedes a judgment.
But a critic's analysis entails subjectivity,
an opinion existing in the mind,
never elsewhere.

Moreover, a critic will claim to serve
as a counselor, not reporting her private
pleasures, but advising others on the likelihoods
that they will gain pleasure from partaking.

Fundamentally, a critic ministers
as a faultfinder of her own mind,
a censurer of her own sentience,
a caricaturist of her own provincialism,
a quibbler of the bean count in her brain,

an apparition projecting her thoughts
into the nerve networks of another.

I tell this to my wife.
She thinks I make suggestions.

CORPORAL COUNSELOR

As I strolled across our town's tiny sidewalk,
gently harried by a flurry of snowflakes
heralding October, a stranger drew nearer to me,
as though he sought to warm his hands.
A wooly hat topped his head like a bison bouffant.
His boots were meant for winter's carpet,
and this day might render one. Frosty fumes

escaped his lips like a chimney's pulsing spume.
His gaze revealed an acquaintance with my thinly
layered silhouette, and he marked my wardrobe
spoke of August, as though I turned the clock aside.
I suspected he only stopped to take advantage
of my windbreak, upstream of the snowy flow.
His bare hands parked outside his coat pockets,

as I hoisted mine in wary greeting. The half-familiar
face emerged from his wraps. His breath reeked
of stale tobacco, though I'd never seen him
at the roadhouse where I drank my evening meals.
He spoke my name musically, in a manner customarily
delivered as an overture to a prolonged rendezvous,
not merely frothy chitchat. I combed the catacombs

of my memory, searching for rehearsed remarks
appropriate for those rare episodes when earnest
conversation cannot be dodged by routine guile.
"Why so steamy on this freshly frosted day?" I said.
He bobbed his head as though wrenching my words
upward to disperse in the continuum of clouds.
He snatched the reins of our dialogue.

Indeed, a monologue emerged.
"Hank," said he, "I'll get it off my chest.
I'm not much good at speeches, but I'm vigilant
when a better man preaches. You know, when you
spoke up at the Men's Bible Study Group? About you?
It hit a nerve in me. It was like you were talking
for myself, as well. That man you exposed, well,

"that same man gallivants as the duplicate of me.
You told about a Christmas Eve when Christian hymns
caroled through our streets. You said you couldn't feel
the sacred singing anymore this year. You glared at
choir members and witnessed only fraud. Each singer
stood pretending to glorify God. Each face you saw
felt to you as foreign as the outskirts of the moon.

"Each eye, each nose, each cheek revealed
a hideous head that didn't resemble you.
In the mirrored glass of your windowpane,
you witnessed the anathema you'd become. You said,
'In my isolation, I've escaped from all Mankind.'

Everyone you encountered seemed a villain wrapped
in the robes of rectitude. Every successful specimen

"just got lucky, or else, they knew someone. None
had earned their prize. Phonies flourish on this planet.
You despised this world of grift where even Christians
playact their roles. You told how an angel hovered
then on your chandelier and held her mirror for you
to gaze upon the jealous monster you'd become.
In a tearful convulsion, you despised your graceless life.

"You said, 'Lord, I've beaten gluttony and so nearly
conquered lust. I trampled greed, sloth, and wrath.
I sanctify your Name. No other gods tempt my respect.
I regard the sabbath holy. My parents are my guides.
I've never murdered, only in my mind. No adultery will
ensnare me, nope, never, not again. I couldn't steal
a penny. A lie would make me sick. But Lord,

"'I can't dodge the two sins that mark this age.
I swim within a cesspool of putrefying pride.
I've sunk into the quicksand of envy's suicide.'
Then you bolted out the door and seized upon
your station in this flawed nation. You sniffed
a barbershop's discarded tresses. You licked
a mailman's face. You tasted blood that dripped

"from a housemaid's kitchen wound. You saw
the soldier limp. You felt a cancer patient's pain.
You tore off your shirt and slapped your breast

and cried, 'This heartbeat drums in you.' Though
the shoppers in the grocery store appeared
bemused, you howled, 'At last, I arise, a man again,
one fleck from Mankind's crown.' Well, Hank,

"I need to thank you. You ripped my blindfold off.
I think I've licked my own arrogance and jealousy,
a little, because you shared your own conquest
of these beasts. I guess the Lord sent me you,
my guardian angel, because the rest were all busy,
way upstairs. I wanted to tell you face-to-face
that your layman's preaching put me in my place.

"I've stolen too much of your time, and, well,
that's all I got to say." In a moment, he vanished
in the snowfall, like a raindrop in the sea. The memory
of that chance encounter in chilly October returns
when snowflakes waft like tatters of angelic thoughts.
I recall my visitor's words, and I try to feel a bond
of brotherly love with him. That ephemeral epiphany

swirls in the frozen white flecks. But two predators,
pride and envy, pounce upon you from the mists.
You evict them, quite successfully, but leave
a door ajar, and so these monsters leap back inside.
A moment later, every neighbor is a faker,
a phony who got lucky, unworthy of his gain,
never to know of your superiority. But I will recall

that random meeting, the happenstance, perhaps
a predestined collision with my own guardian angel
in the tumbling veil of snow on a smalltown sidewalk.
I ponder his victory over his selfish self. Somehow,
he saw through my sin to spot the bedfellow within.
Praise a man for his failure—his failure to succeed
at immaculate vanity. He loved my divine failure.
And, God help me, let me love the same in him.

ONE SOUL

My quintessence knocked
upon the door of a cupboard
in my cranial kitchen.
All my cups kept quiet, out of touch.

Something hungry out there
wrote me into the soup.
I got bit; I got gobbled.
My pith persists, still a cavity unknown.

Inside an atom's gallery
resides a behemothic blank,
an essence sent to ingest me,
the ethos of a soul.

COLLEGE

A fiesta of freedom, a cauldron of smoldering fire,
a college confronts the wannabes, but not-evers,
with their trifling substance, but jumbo desire
for a serious selfhood, for a meritorious name.
Such aspirations readily thrive in our trade schools
where vocations are taught, and employers hire
those engaging in entrepreneurial endeavors,
but few collegiates exchange college credits for fame.
An elusive dream of esteem requires marketable tools.

A BABY'S BIRTH

Do unborn babies weigh the pain and gain
of launching emigration? Some remain
extinct, cantankerous contrarians,
rebuffing Good Samaritans
who labor, gruelingly, to liberate
those elves—serene, quite satisfied, to date,
with fate's fortuitous environment,
a habitat maintaining sure content.
A shove, a squeeze, and chaos detonates.
An audience, agape, arrives and rates
the getaway as grand, a thunderbolt.
One wonders why these pampered imps revolt,
renouncing lavish mansions, seeking proofs
of cellar doors and paradisal roofs.

AN ACT OF KINDNESS

She'd never liked their nationality,
their ethnicity, their tribe, their clan.
One member manifests their entirety
and simplifies the baggage scan.

Then, one day, an act of kindness
bestowed to her, by one of them,
unraveled her analysis. Blindless
looms outside a halo's hem.

A broken brick can fell a wall,
but every masonry arose
from single stones, too small,
too light, to glorify in prose.

The episode reshaped her mind.
Who knew about these superpowers!
Mightier than pen or sword, the kind
raise stems below the flowers.

GET WELL CARDS (CALIBRATED)

Get Well Soon!
Praying for your rapid recovery
at 100% your incredible self!

Get Well Soon!
So, Doc says, "You're getting better,
each day, but these injuries are slow healers."
Well, towering at 90%,
you're still smoking the clouds.

Get Well Soon!
The hospital chart claims your vitals
vacillate, around 80%. Four-fifths
of a legend won't tarnish your myth.

Get Well Soon!
You feel maybe 70%? That's two-thirds
of the impossible saga your life authored.

Get Well Soon!
Your family reported you're at 60%.
Heck, that's over half! If I had your health,
I'd be seventeen.

Get Well Soon!
Halfway back, according to you.
Say, superman, donate the other 50%
to some army,
the one on *our* side! (ha ha)

Get Well Soon!
I heard you still muster 40% of your vigor.
No need to be greedy.
You've still got more stamina
than our whole executive team.

Get Well Soon!
For some, 30% of their strength
would prove an impediment.
For you, it's merely a desirable diet,
shedding the excess mass
of exorbitant energy.

Get Well Soon!
Though your physician informs us
you retain 20% of your prowess
(only for now, not going forward)
in performing activities of daily living,
who needs to shower, anyway?
It's about time someone took
care of you for a while, after years
of service, saving the day over here.

Get Well Soon!
At 10% of yourself, one-tenth
of your extravagant essence,
you're way overqualified
to work here in our office.
You've transcended the mundane.
Let lesser lights assist you
in eating or using the john.

Get Well Soon!
The medical staff warns me
of a 0% chance this card
will reach you in time. Ask
for a second opinion, and,
if you want mine, I presume
you will outlive us all.
Please keep in touch,
wherever your future
adventures usher you.
Though your whisper now wafts
softer, your ghostly murmur
still enlightens my mind.
As you know, we've got
dozens of deadwood,
heirloom employees,
beneficiaries of nepotism,
over here at the office.
Whether you know it or not,

you've already returned
in your ethereal pajamas.
And what a pleasure
to work with a legacy
employee who actually carries
his own weight around here!

JONAH AND THE GREAT FISH

River Leviathan, a legend, the sturgeon,
big as a man and hungry as wolves,
slithers silently upon bottom mud
of northland's mightiest fresh waters,
flowing in search of their falling's finale.

I'd battled this beast in River St. Croix.
Three hours we'd fought that summer,
when silence surrounded our bedlam.
Birds watched from cliffs of this aquatic
arena, watching to see which would win

this saga, this brawl, between fisher and fished.
Chained but untamed, this behemothic beast
drew nearer, then nearer, near to my boat.
I wrestled the demon from its depth in the deep.
Half submarine, half snake, the creature fought

me below, but what finality awaited, I'd soon come
to know, for the devil's skull surfaced, biting
my boat, portending to gnaw each object it saw.
Hugging this horror, I wrangled it into my bare
boatful of dry floor atop the St. Croix's wild waves.

Our demonic dance, cheek to cheek, thrashing
and writhing, convulsed my small river craft,

and I foresaw I'd submerge and enroll in its realm
below us, where St. Croix's jungle juice flows.
But as I guzzled the air, the beast imbibed naught

but listless annihilation as tick after tock, the gas
in its gills fizzled to an unceremonious stop.
Yet I couldn't slacken my embrace of this beast.
I clutched it as if its vitality seeped into my skin,
as though the struggle's cessation awakened

the breaths gushing from me, as though
the heartbeats within the four chambers
of my corporeal pump paused to adjust
and acclimatize the outlandish soul I'd usurped.
Two hawks sailed in step with the river's flow,

seeming to tear one page from this chapter,
for this spasmatic story jarred to its climax,
wrenching ahead to its next launch. Blood pooled
in the boat's hull. The sturgeon had nearly severed
my arm, and my thumb slept in its gullet.

No physician fancied my left arm worth salvaging.
I rebuffed all advisements on prosthetic replacement.
For months, my fiery passions smoldered.
Vainly, I struggled to name the source of my fury.
I conceptualized some creature tormenting

the tenderest dendrites decorating my brain.
Some oppressive force, some tyrannical power

sought to subjugate me. This vexatious thing,
this nameless despot, intruded upon the sanctity
of selfhood, of self-rule, of soul's sovereignty.

Next summer, newspapers along the Canadian border
reported the astounding rumors of rampage.
"The Rainy River Wraith," so named by paper and ink,
slaughtered a swimmer, beheaded a bather,
and harassed fishermen's boats from a touristy lodge.

This creature embodied that nebulous nether-thing
that afflicted the rightful repose I'd always known.
In fury, I fancied this troll swam Rainy River solely
to taunt me, to flaunt reign over me. Its cruel clout
wobbled the cobblestones upholstering my brain.

I arrived at the Baudette resort. My lodge room
boasted a view of the river, as I insisted it must.
The waterway twinkled. A trillion candles flashed
in each exuberant instant of life. Beneath this fiery
watery plane, a levitation prowled, the Wraith.

Most active at sundown, this satanic sturgeon,
by some preternatural stealth, perceived I'd arrived.
Else, why did my cranial conflagration subside?
We two knew, as a candlewick knows its puddle of wax,
on this twilight, two of us tussle; one of us dies.

The lodge arranged for my boat, rod, reel, and hook.
But I eschewed their meager selection of bait.

A local insider betrayed his closely guarded secret,
when I overheard in the hallway of his discovery
of gargantuan earthworms that lurked in the woods,

just behind this lodge. I clawed with fingernails,
ones attached to my right arm, though the stump
on my left prickled and itched, as though longing
to delve into this ditch in the dark. I finally exhumed
a fistful of red angleworms, night crawlers, squirming,

twisting, meandering pinkies, with hundreds of rings
on each finger, as though wedded to dozens of brides.
Why not? These hermaphrodites each carry five hearts.
Yet none of these earthworms sufficed. At ten inches
or so, they bestowed scant scraps as hors d'oeuvres

hooked for the Wraith of the River. At last, I grasped
the slithering slinker I sought. Again and again, he
struggled to slide back to his black sanctuary.
Finally, I wrapped him around my trembling arm,
all three feet of him careening and convulsing around.

Said I, "I fancy you'd serve as a surrogate arm,
but your mission awaits at the end of a hook."
Said he, "I won't go. Leave me alone. I know
of the evil, the Wraith. No persuasion from me
could provoke its conversion to sturgeon piety."

Said I, "How so? Just trust my guidance and go."
Said he, "Such a hazardous assignment for me,

but easy for you to dictate and decree as a godhead.
I'm too young to die. I've a family, you know, well—
just me, but I'll not die to soothe your insanity."

Said I, "Earthworms suffer from a dearth of identity,
nameless, aimless, spineless, and cold. Be bold.
I christen thee *Jonah*. 'Tis Jonah I choose to right
wrongs of the Wraith, to face a seemingly certain
demise. Trust me. You've no choice. You're chosen."

At midnight, my boat rippled the rims of Rainy River.
Mists nestled the moon, and my fingers felt wet
as I loaded Jonah on the immaculate hook.
A five-ounce sinker secured my long arcing cast
to the rocky cellar where bottom-feeders dwell.

When Jonah plunged to the floor of the river,
a mighty tug on the line roused bells in my brain.
The Wraith swallowed Jonah whole, end-to-end.
Matters progressed, swimmingly, according to plan.
I'd chosen Jonah for his quick mind, his brevity,

his talent to explain complexity with lucidity,
his uncanny capacity to persuade, to prevail,
where blowhards, tattlers, and blabbermouths fail.
From the maw of the Wraith, Jonah harangued.
Said he, "Repent ere anon, or the river reverses."

For every sturgeon forebodes one inescapable fact:
what flows to the left must one day flow back

to the right. Jonah proclaimed what the Wraith
knew in truth. Furthermore, the Wraith understood
that heralds, doomsayers, ones with big mouths,

invariably get backing from Someone above,
exercising big muscles. The Wraith repented
remorsefully of its misadventures and pledged
to evermore practice proper precepts of the fishery,
ambushing crustaceans and fish smaller than men.

The Wraith vomited Jonah, and I reeled in that worm.
When I heaved him aboard, he looked bitter,
even angry, as though harboring a grudge. Said he:
"Why'd you have to use *me*? And *who* made *you* Judge!
You could've wrestled the Wraith far better than me!"

Said I, "As a worm, you've articulated the mystery
menacing men, the consummate inquiry, a paramount
puzzle. I lent you my own name to second your query."
We don't wish to go where the Lord sends us. We wail,
"Why do *You* need *me*?" God enrolls us in creative acts.

FAMILIES

No tomcat sought to claim a wife.
No hound dog sought its son.
No beast foresees the end of life,
once heartbeats have begun.
A creature's family
forms arbitrarily,
amidst whomever they outrun.

In Man and beast, congruities
perhaps insinuate
both families form entities
that often abdicate
their duties to perform
as shelter from the storm,
when lighthouse rays revolve too late.

But Man refutes a beast's pantomime,
for one important reason.
God's favored primate treasures Time,
while beasts enjoy one season.
Familial bonds revive
when memories arrive.
Our bygones censure future's treason.

A family's eternal clock
wields Time's infinitude,
as manifested by their flock,
an endless interlude
of morrows. Yesterday's
agendas rose to raise
fresh faith from bygone rectitude.

UNCLE SCHOOL

You learned of straight and narrow paths
in Sunday school: *Walk righteous roads!*
From me, you feared the aftermaths.
You'll carry grief in wagonloads.

High schoolers learn a victor's pose,
but you're well-versed in infamy,
from watching me as I arose,
a scofflaw of sobriety.

Your parents painted paragons
upon your retinas—portrayed
exemplars running marathons—
to show just how perfection's played.

If sorrow flowered fatally,
my hearse would flaunt a garden grove.
If failure could emphatically
incinerate, I'd light a stove

and brandish fire's leftover heat
to torch my dreams, my schemes, my vice,
inside my shack on Loser Street,
wherein I'd never sacrifice

one moment's lethargy to plan
ahead for fond futurity.
Epitomizing wayward Man,
I manifest buffoonery.

So said, I serve as mentor, coach,
advisor, guiding juveniles.
My nephews cringe when I approach.
Revulsion animates my smiles.

Without my bad example, too,
who would fortify their do-and-don't?
Despite abundant family glue,
kids often slide, but thanks to me, they won't.

BIBLE UNDERSTUDY (LUKE 23: 42–43)

Our church's Christmas pageant recruits
parishioners, amateur actors to play
the roles of wise men and shepherds,
gentle souls who humbly journeyed
to Bethlehem. We feel comfortable as
understudies in this biblical drama. Since
we don't engage in dialogues, the script
requires only standing around and loving
this miraculous God child, the cynosure
and savior in our Lord's divine plan.

We Lutherans believe deeply, but quietly.
Serenity affords the perfect match for God's
peace. Why go around babbling a bunch
of admonitions when our tranquility articulates
what you're missing? Stoic, taciturn Scandinavians
populate the North Star State. Superfluous
words reveal weakness, a failure in fortitude,
meager stamina, insufficient self-sufficiency.
Moreover, the garrulous, loquacious, gabby
meddlers seek only an audience, not conversation.

This winter, one newcomer to our church suggested
a more dynamic Easter pageant, wherein we erect

three crosses near the altar. The middle one would bear a Christ statue. No one would presume to imitate Him. But townsfolk could take turns as the two thieves, getting lightly nailed to flanking crosses for sham crucifixions. Most of us would play the penitent thief, but the other, doubting, mocking thief might get portrayed by some scofflaws downtown. At first, we, the church council, felt appalled,

but later, we began to warm up to the idea, especially since we wouldn't need to say too much, and probably, we could get away with some heartfelt ad-libbing because there's a minimal script. You don't even want to read about a real crucifixion. It's torture beyond the boundaries of nightmares. But by seeking to suffer a dab of discomfort, we'd get jarred into grasping what Christ did. God's Son canceled the penalties for our sins. Now we believers belong to Him. The physical world always felt unreal to me.

Now Heaven seems obvious. That penitent thief on the cross embodies the luckiest guy in history. Memorize his lines: "Jesus, remember me when you come into your kingdom." It sounds like a hopeless, desperate plea from a thief who was likely a better man than I ever was. But this guy found faith in an immaculate Man. I think everyone intuitively knows that Good exists somewhere suffusing the cosmos. And everyone knows Man is intrinsically Bad. Imagine hanging on a cross, waiting to die, and by a stunning stroke of luck, witnessing Good abruptly manifest Itself a few steps away. Trust me, you'd find faith when that happened. And you'd say, "Remember me," not even so much to be saved, but more to enjoy the eternal bliss of loving Him, of finally leaping into the Good. You awaited till your hour of death to hear words you can finally believe.

"Truly, I say to you, today you will be with me in Paradise."

I'm a quiet man. But at this year's Easter pageant, I'm talking.

HIS FAMILY

His family resided here.
Which house he owned remains unclear.
They all look alike in winter snow.
The Great Depression ruined that year.

We watched his son and daughter grow,
as local heroes, people know.
They got their brains from Ma, some say.
Connectiveness gets hard to show.

I'd met that man one Saturday.
As summer hands, we plowed for pay.
He seemed as wild and free as me,
then he got married late in May.

At first, the house held he and she.
A girl arrived when two makes three.
When number four was nearly due,
I knew he'd changed excessively.

A family bestows the glue
to gently reinforce what's true.
He sat in church some Sundays too.
Them kids can make a man of you.

THE MACHINE-LEARNING FAMILY

Families resemble an electronic device,
storing, retrieving, and processing pieces,
reassembling the puzzle from each fugitive slice.

Families metamorphose as pliant machines,
intelligent contraptions, ignorant gadgets,
with adaptability stuffed in their genes.

Parent and child begin unaware
of their future, of unforeseen, flexible facts.
Algorithmic disputes invariably flare.

Machine learning improves with more data.
Input and response, anger and yelling,
these sentiments sediment in a family's strata.

A model behavior arises from family affairs,
predicting reactions in family dyads.
But new data emerge to rejigger the pairs.

Families fit data in formulas, meticulous math,
but no training, no validation, no community input
can prepare you to predict your family's path.

Families who flourish know families act strange,
as machines seeking a desirable output,
the simplest solutions, and a fair error range.

PRAY CASUALLY

Be still, and know that I am God. ~ Psalm 46:10

Hovering, fluttering, flickering, God's realm
overwhelms
your pondering, wondering—ushering rescue
from you.

Through bone, past flesh, across wits,
faith flits,
slumbering, gathering, thundering your shouts,
with doubts.

Then the poetry ends.

I've tried to squeeze my brain into submission.
I sought a deeper faith, a corporeal bridge to Christ.
But our brains deceive us, imagining they can
perform miracles. After all, we work hard to achieve
anything else, but the harder my brain labors
at ligatures, the farther I drift from Him. I reasoned
that my arduous attempts at snatching Him would
prove the sole road to success. I focused frantically
on erecting that bridge from bricks in my brain.

But the soul suffuses a refuge outside the solitary
confinement in our fleshy penitentiaries. At quiet

casual moments, you find His presence patiently
parked on the outskirts of your skullcap's small town,
and your village nestles in the valley of Heaven.
Imagine your nonchalance when viewing the moon.
Recall your composure when feeling the breeze.
Fancy the ease you felt when hearing a birdsong.
At peace, you felt no surprise, no confusion, no need
to analyze. If I labor at prayer, I know I'm doing
it wrong. Prayers bubble in your other brain bucket.

Don't pray for an invitation. You're at the party.
Pray casually.
Pray like you're already there.

A LITTLE LIGHT

Sun glare buries our blue skies.
A little light will suffice.
But God's Light blinds,
a dazzling deliverance,
springing open the cabinets
and caskets of stored memories.

My private shadow repeats me.
If I were a tree, my shadow
would shade,
wheeling a dark skeleton,
dragged by the sun.
Trees whisper.

I remember that sound,
morning murmurs of parents,
as I lay in my bed,
watching the whispering light
creep under the door.
I've forgotten the details

of every book that I've read.
I recall only the idea,
the notion, the warmth.
I stroll past a graveyard,

where all my rivals await
our reunion.

We fought over trifles.
We battled for baubles,
hoarding smoke from the fire.
I hope for the hour
when I and my bitterest foe,
arm-in-arm, advance into Heaven.

PART V:
the wild

MOOSE HEAD

Pierre Verendrye's mounted moose head greeted me
on each visit to his rustic tavern, a hunter's eatery.

The beast perched atop a crackling fireplace
whose blaze bedazzled the barroom's furriest face,

within a whimsical dance of a flickering flame.
Staccato clinks of beer mugs sometimes became

indistinguishable from the snaps of burning wood.
The moose roused the aura of Pierre's neighborhood.

After salting, pickling, and tanning the skin,
the taxidermist contrived a contemptuous grin

on the moose to animate his protruding muzzle,
as though his immortality provoked a fresh puzzle

that he lacked the leisure to contemplate before.
Domineering glass eyes outstared each bar carnivore.

Pierre said, "Our own heads ain't fit for no trophies.
Else, I'd rack all your scalps in my menageries."

Pierre moved the moose head above the bar door.
Boots drummed make-believe hoofbeats over the floor.

But Nature's Wild withers inside trafficked spaces.
Places beget specimens. Specimens forget places.

The moose missed the bedlam of bestial creatures.
He forecasts our phantoms will soon beget features.

ARROWHEAD NORTHERN LIGHTS

The state map sculpts this land's mission.

Behold Minnesota's menacing spire,
the northeastern corner's big bayonet,
a gargantuan arrowhead scraping the sky,
raking the rims of night's radiant vault,
slitting the hems of the heavens,
lancing the lining at the eeriest boundary

between the earth and the elsewhere.
The lustrous blush of a borderland drizzles
the ghostly green bloom of a foreign frontier.
A garden alights to overwhelm retinal realms,
in glowing phantasms of chromatic complexions,
in luminous streamers of celestial sailors.

The ragged black horizon of trees
roosts like a platter, hoisting the writhing,
alien scenery. Kaleidoscopes bathe in a rink
of spilt ink, aloft in the inscrutable high.
Look north for night's spectacle, the inferno,
an advancing cosmos on fire, an aurora borealis.

The conflagration embraces the rippling lids
of the lakes, greeting the flares in the air.
Emerald ribbons sway over watery precincts,

dancing, meandering in a delirious romp.
The firestorm arises to the brink of cognition.
Convocations of color peek through the cracks.

The firmament bursts without whispers,
and an arena ignites without murmurs.
This theater seethes, but no luminosity sighs.
Our grandstand smolders in silent narration.
Arrowhead Lights blaze in a voiceless volcano,
a shrieking quintessence of quietude.

THE WHIRLING SQUIRREL

Whirling, squirming, fidgeting, the turf
sprouts a finger, so it seems, foraging,
scavenging Earth's elusive veneer.

Quickly, contemplating destiny,
springing, grasping boughs of evergreens,
its life arrives in treetops, always stormily.

Branches dance, gesticulating joy.
Exhilaration bursts over the quivering wood.
Needles splatter, raining giddy, green,

vivified confetti upon languid grass,
hushed when the fleeting fervors soon pass.
Tapping, chatting, pattering, the sprite

leaps to lofty pinnacles, a hound
hectoring the sky and badgering
clouds adrift in remote serenity.

A detonation dispatching delirium,
it flares through the boughs,
limbs still alit from bark to sap to pith.

Find the sylvan imp a-sailing, bright,
brash, a kite arousing ecstasy,
soaring avian abodes, in flight,

floating fearlessly to dynamize
rhapsodies in neighboring trees,
then leaving leaf and limb abandoned,

freed utterly from bounce and buoyancy.
Raising arms to resemble a tree,
I imagine passion pounce upon me.

WIND IN THE NORTHLAND PINES

When northern pines unhook their spines,
and birch bequeath their teeth
to thieves so sly, they dodge your eye,
find cruel designs in air's affairs.

None know where apparitions go.
None understand their plan.
None find a face grace anyplace
where its brandished hands command.

Winds deputize those visualized
to speak their creaking tale.
Let firs confirm their meddling wings.
Let oaks announce their strokes.

Let thistles' whistle puff epistles.
Let tamaracks unpack
the phantom anthem's melody,
a specter's hectoring hymn.

Though Norway pines recite their lines,
the author wafts in drafts.
The boughs awake for crosswinds' sake,
and rattle tattling tunes.

A forest fancies freedom's prancing
when skinned by wanton wind.
Then the wraith renounced its fleeting faith.
The bitter breeze blew leafy litter,

pursuing wind's ensuing quest
to find the forest's door.
The wind rescinded breezing breaths
and died from suicide.

GOPHER GRAVEYARDS

Ponder this prowler, the beast in the basement,
the burrower under our surface terrain,
nibbling the roots of our manicured landscapes,
a hermit hectoring the carpeted plain,
a pillager prince, in subterranean reign.

Gnawers, not kissers, its lips hide beneath teeth,
never smooching a sweetheart, never complaining
of its misanthropic existence, its solitaire cottage,
ever shunning sun showers, never explaining
what manifesto or myth it's maintaining.

The miner of topsoil's treasure, a bounteous sod,
the shoveler of mud, a spry spade underground,
it tunnels the floorboards of Earth, its ceiling,
ostentatiously flaunting the dirt that it's found,
pound after pound, in a mountainous mound.

Despite ravaging grasses and gardens and trees,
it fancies itself Earth's engineer, aerating a subway,
improving Earth's drainage, opening deep doors
in the cellar, in the sand and the silt and the clay,
laboring every hour, work undistinguished from play.

Then ponder its wisdom, its sagacious foresight.
We who parade in a sunny, wind-weathered conclave

forget fortunes soon fade and alight black as night.
Credit this creature, living all alone in its cave,
never exalting the sun, never fearing the grave.

The wise gopher knows you're dead a long time.
Why strive to perfect your ephemeral sunny-side cheer?
In the end, we're all jailed for the same corporeal crime.
Dig, tunnel, and burrow, year after year,
till your crypt's optimal fit lays lovingly near.

MINNESOTA WILDLAND

If Minnesota wildness pounced to smite
the city dwellers, cozily debased
in futile, bureaucratic blatherskite,
they'd flee their minnesota, lowercased.

Renounce these ruling, regulating 'crats.
True Minnesotans romp as savagely
as forest cats, as eagle acrobats.
Keep Minnesota rapturously free.

A wildness prods the pith of northland folks.
We're wild as walleyes, lording over lakes.
We're moose and bear and lightning's thunderstrokes.
We're snowdrifts, feral, fit, no flitting flakes.

Save nature—yes, *man's* nature—undefiled.
Away from cities' cesspools, men rise wild.

FAKE FIREFLIES

In random retinal prickles,
a rambling firefly tickles
our eyes' electrical sickles.

A taciturn lantern fly,
ever and never nearby,
both audacious and shy,

a winking spark in twilight,
a toy star tumbled to grass height,
begins etching lightning in flight.

With glints of flickering fame,
the flashes of fleeting acclaim,
his candle's blink will inflame

a beetle belle's dream,
tinged with theatrical esteem,
enrolled in Nature's inscrutable scheme.

Then moths encircle a streetlamp's flare
and snatch fire from its radiant glare.
Tiny torches appear to dance in the air.

When credible credentials prove fake,
phony flies can glow as their genuine namesake,
with history's homage and our survival at stake.

BEAVERS

If you carry a chair atop of your butt,
and squint tiny eyes, both nearly shut,
and brandish your buckteeth's timber cleavers,
we're believers. You personify beavers.

A philosophical quandary perpetually dangles.
You deliberate, then assess all the angles.
You've toppled a tree. But now what?
Refurbish your hut or garnish your gut?

You're torn between an act and a feat,
two tasks, to wit: *Shall I build? Shall I eat?*
A log evinces vittles. A log begets a ceiling.
Your den excites an epicurean feeling.

The biggest rodents still around, beavers
loot as hooligans, demonic overachievers,
harboring disdain for the public domain.
Each birch's plummet heralds their gain.

Like every creature, beavers exist solely
to ravish the earth, in rampages, holy
or unholy, in egomaniacal pillage,
building their shack, wrecking a village,
rationing a river's lifesaving spillage.

These rodents never render one thought
of the ruination their revelries wrought.
Yet beavers accidentally spring up as heroes,
confounding the blundering government bureaus.
Dams restore wetlands. Thank these miserly zeros.

Dams balance the bombast of aquatic microbial gangs.
Dams smooth the flow of groundwater's boomerangs.
Frogs and waterfowl enter as tourists each spring.
But beavers bemoan the benevolence they bring.
They sought havoc as brutes, serving a merciless king.

They sought to sequester the river's wet wealth
to succor their safety, to foster their health.
But Mother Nature ever fashions her schemes
to improvise chaos, as much more than it seems,
unlatching the doorways dribbling her dreams.

LIGHTNING'S RETURN STROKES

After clouds discharge electricity,
the earth surpasses their mendacity.

The luminosity of lightning bolts, what we see,
arises on Earth's return strokes, visibly.

Provoke this planet? Arouse her pique?
Punch her nose? She'll slap your cheek,

hurling bolts to make the cloud ogres shake.
Colossal titans up there cause the deafening quake.

Then hear the thunderous tumbling wall.
The proud perch highest whenever they fall.

PEOPLE'S PRECINCTS. NATURE'S QUARTERS

The day her baby died, Nature embraced
her sorrow. She detected doors ajar
and Nature's vapors ferrying an unfamiliar life.

Her prior times, now displaced, steamed
and fled, like bubbles arisen to the brim
to burst atop the boiling pot.

Silent snowfall, clear and cold, arose.
She entered another space,
a frosty, impartial precinct, abandoning

disillusionment. Loss liberates the loser.
An anchor lifts. The ship dives into the deep.
She drifts in a lost lifeboat.

Outside, in Nature's Quarters,
radiance arose, reflected on a river.
Sparkles winked in a jubilant sequence,

tapping a code known in Nature's arena.
Ebullient trees gossiped. Birch and aspen
rattled tambourines. Elm and willow

swapped photonic epistles,
so swiftly that the ricochets
of the sun's tidings bounced

without any rat-a-tat arriving
from each rapturous rap.
A serene breeze meandered

as an inquisitive cat,
aware we beheld her,
aware we witnessed her joy.

INTO THE WOODS

I awoke as the ghost of October, a specter
sprung from the cumbrance of slumber.
On that macabre morn,
borne in the calm of an autumn,
the wild woods menaced me.

On each new morning, they'd advanced
a meter or so, encroaching my cabin.
I'd tied a red scarf on one vagabond birch,
just last night. Out of my sight, the red wrap
leapt to an aspen, as though taunting me,

for they knew that I knew, the glossy white
trunk of an aspen flaunts black stripes
like a birch, but only aspens are scarred
with scabs, those black knotty eyes
watching me, appraising me from artful angles.

Through my window, they pulsed as a presence.
A swathe of aspen glistened in dollops of dawn.
A tiny breeze brushed the heart-patterned leaves,
and wood witches whispered to me, me alone.
A birch branch scratched my window, and soon

the glass shattered, seemingly leaping at me,
from a capricious decision in response to a dare.

In ominous echoes, all panes in my rustic domain
crackled like struck stones, tinkled like wind chimes,
and sought to sit on my carpet as primeval sand.

Long logs laced my cabin. These tame trunks
trembled and struggled to rise, collapsing the roof,
just as I rolled out the door. My home nestled no more
as a port in the forest. I rose, cast in the carriage
of a sailor lost at sea, an ocean of wildest woods.

My place in Time
hopped back
a thousand years.
I returned to Big Woods
of erstwhile Minnesota, a rudimentary bygone.

Yet October nuzzled
my fragile skin.
My daintiness awed me.
I stroked the nearest
barked beast,

a giant white wood leg,
yet alive, dynamic
within. A hidden
ebullience bustled,
secreted from my senses.

Straight as a laser,
the trunk launched

to the sky, refusing
to brush the sodden
soot of the clouds.

Up, up, at the top,
the leafy gold flag
fluttered, as an anthem
to autumn, fireworks
frozen in time.

A fragrance roused
remembrance of seasons,
the celestial seesaw
churning the circle
of bountiful birth.

Man's remains decay
monstrously. Yet I inhaled
a gala of glory,
sniffing the story
of aspens' savory leaves.

Yellow paws, unhooked
from the branches,
hovered, suspended
in air, sprinkling
a lemony breeze.

Aspen and birch shared
their perch, all parallel

to their mates, all perpendicular
to the soft amber carpet
that leaves bequeathed to my boots.

Like a drawerful of combs,
the trees stood scrambled,
resembling the mane of a giant,
or the grooming tool
that the leviathan sought.

The birch trunks felt like stone
to my touch. Yet some say
they soar as the softest of trees,
seeking only to gift their pulpwood
as paper, paging our books.

The yellow pavement
glistened with dew.
Birch and aspen—who knew
which cast aside paddings
leapt from which branch?

Clumps of aspens
betrayed the wiles
of their roots, raising
clones, nearest neighbors,
inbred families, not a romance happenstance.

We, too, wish for apartness,
but strangers encroach

the perimeter
of our desired address,
discreet and sequestered.

The heavenward spines
of each bole stood
as stoic as nails, heedless
of the heavenly hammer
perpetually poised overhead.

Immobile as soldiers
on guard, watchful,
vigilant, sentinels
gentle as toy troopers,
these titans of timber

sojourned as sentries,
a century or two,
standing in wait
for the unseen events
happening now.

A few obscure shrubs tangled
the scenery. Their green leaves
dangled inches above
emerald moss at the base
of the ascending white birch

and the soft yellow carpet.
Convulsive contrasts

between these too vivid colors
assailed the gray in my brain.
They flashed yes or no, stop or go.

At the pinnacles of these mottled,
white spires, a sparse golden
foliage shivered in a breeze
too benign to loot the last leaves,
which rattled their steadfast regrets.

Sunbeams scattered at the whim
of the wind, as the billowing foliage
rotated the rays, casting a whirling,
twirling, pirouetting skeleton of light.
The sun's searchlights crisscrossed

the woods as ghostly gold beams
that braced the frame of the forest.
The trimmed canopy above afforded
just the right light. I fancied the treetops
as an artist's brush sketching the sky's mural.

A forest floor begets a glorious mess.
No dustbin or broom ever embellished
its beauty. A recent rain emboldened
the blooms of fern and fungi. Rotting
things flaunt their dainty bouquet in the forest.

Littering their lost lives, the forest things
carpet their castle with memories.

My boots snapped the threads of this rug
with each footfall. Each aspen stared at
its siblings, perhaps in the midst of a family fight.

Lichens mastered the menagerie of symbiosis,
the confederacy of algae and fungi,
on thick, rough bark of newly jeweled trees.
Nature broadcasts its conspiracies,
while my microbiome slinks in deep crypts.

The edge of the woods ever scares us,
more than does whatever awaits in its bowels.
Just so, each orifice we brandish fails
to forecast the pleasures within.
Secrets seem sinister.

The face of the woods
stands as an unfinished wall,
porous perhaps—but penetrable?
Our minds envisage a trap.
The woods tease with a peek,

not a grandiose gaze
on prospective trails.
The mask of the woods
taunts the timid
who aspire to enter

through the striped ramparts,
into the bristles of beards,

caught in the camouflage,
adding human disorder
to a forest's dark disarray.

But just before winter,
the forest floor landscape
spreads as a blanket.
The woodland's radiant canopy
tumbles in lavish confetti,

the beautiful bedsheets
that herald the seasonal sleep.
Walk on the quilt till you repose
below it. Trees tower like streetlights,
with no lamp alit—none we can see.

Nude woods look safer.
None know the woods' wardrobe.
The naked don't murder.
No highwaymen disrobe
before robbing. Yet the edge

of the woods dresses up
at the doorstep, in a wrapper,
a ribbon, a scarf, a shawl,
of patchwork gingham,
houndstooth, and paisley patterns.

Thick threads, layers of lumber,
interlace the palisade's textile.

Boughs sprout to dangle the drapery.
The limbs of the mighty arise
to stitch the mosaic canvas.

Tree trunks stand bolt upright,
spikes stretched by the temptation
of Heaven and the tug
of the earth. Each bole
knows its own place, the right space

from its neighbors. Never too near
nor far, the forest things
either agree on the blueprint
in advance, or brutally enforce
the preordained pattern, afterward.

The woods pose in randomness.
So do the machinations of men.
I fancy God placed the trees
in forests as a model to guide
the conduct of Man's social order.

Among countless vertical boles,
each trunk, every branch asserts
ownership of one private space,
one personal mystery, one sacred
mission to live lavishly and die done.

Yet each towering totem honors
obligations to remain in the midst

of the menagerie, the neighborhood
conspiring to storm the galaxy,
overwhelming the patience of prairies.

Here, the sea of trees stretched endlessly
on every side. I felt I bestowed a heart
in this gargantuan body of wood,
the vicious muscle, the swinging door
that opens and closes in concert

with the countless paths proffered
by the forest morass. Through
the ruptured canopy above me,
the sunrise beckoned me, sent me
a summons to travel northeast.

I entered the immobile metropolis
layered with unlit lampposts
and nameless avenues, untitled
to my eyes, though perhaps main streets
and alleys lay known to the woods.

The forest floor litter sat flat,
as if a herd of cattle
munched every shrub, leaving
the fallen leaves to nestle
my footfalls, applauding each step.

The delicate breeze, the woody
whispers, manifested an emotion,

known to their congregation,
heeded by me. Swirls of silence
pumped out, poured into my heart, our heart.

Like jail bars gone bad, the aloft logs
surrounded me in a permeable prison.
Fence poles devoid of barbed wire
granted my dungeon endless escape
routes. Yet each step secured me

as the captive of the timberland stockade,
the jungle jailhouse of a millennium past.
A mouse in the maze, I trudged northeast
among endless flagpoles flinging their fabric,
tossing their bonnets, which fluttered 'round me.

With each step, my casual corral emerged
as a wholly new pen for its livestock, only me,
for all forest beasts fled when I entered their realm.
On my right, a rustle broadcast an adieu of a moose.
To my left, trembling gusts betrayed a bird's launch.

The creatures must know secret doors
renouncing these woods, portals
forbidden to me. I beheld my outlandish
state, foreign to the forest, an alien
among all that belonged here.

At nights, I slept in consummate dark.
Only then would tiny tumults arise

from the tree frogs, crickets, and hooves.
Owls, grasshoppers, and warblers
sang cacophonous chorales roiling my rest.

At last, I surmised they chattered at me,
searched for me, pursued the thing
that I am. I judged my journey now lodged
in my mind. White trunks masqueraded as axons,
electrical cables, the white matter of my brain.

The forest seemed small then. Puddles on the floor
of the forest exposed lakes shrunk for my viewing.
When rainwater dripped from the trees' torn canopy,
I believed a sea leaked from somewhere sublime.
The forest plunged deeper ahead. I left fear behind.

The woods compressed to cuddle my skull,
roosting behind the bones of my forehead,
circling my cerebrum as a dog does his cot,
filling only one cabinet or casket in the nooks
of my knowledge. We composed an alliance.

Trees moved when I moved, snapped like synapses.
Canopy branches splashed their leafy spray
like forested fountains. My shape resembled
the boles, the branches, the foliage,
in an aspen's imagination, in a birch's fantasy.

The buoyant spice of littered leaves,
the refreshing decay of soil-soaked flora,

the delicate dampness breathed
the light touch of its ghosts.
Though trees appear tough, their reveries wobble.

The forest now lingered, lost in my mind.
Just so, I lodged lost in the wondrous woodland.
At last, we found the other, the missing piece,
the axle and wheels, the hoses and valves,
the toggle switch awakening our sentience.

Many, many, more miles northeast, my footfalls
passed red maple trees and orange oaks,
whose crooked skeletons seemed to freeze in a pose
as I approached, as though I served as the judge
of their pageant, as the one they awaited to please.

When evergreens greeted my trek, I knew
great Lake Superior drew near, but my vigor
faltered. I fell to the turf atop the sharp edges
of pinecones and softer caress of scaly spruce fruit.
An underbrush of green needles garlanded my grave.

The pink pouch and white flowers
of a showy lady's slipper perched
next to me, a rare and prized plant.
I reached, then rescinded. I longed
to pluck this sprite by the stem,

as the woods had plucked me,
a delicate, peculiar ornament

in the forest. But let us lie. Let tomorrow,
a millennium hence, mislay our memory.
Supremely awake, we slept seasons.

THE CLAN OF SILENCE

Each racket arises as a singular beast,
an airing of a lone brute in our jungle.
So, too, does each silence surface

as a unique creature, just born,
but an orphan, absent from all
taxonomy charts, indifferent

to any other bygone quietude.
Silence prefers to be alone.
As big as the sea, silence

pours out just one bucket
of stillness upon you at any hour.
One dipperful, only, of silence

splashes on you. Then that drenching
fades and comes not again to anyone.
An impromptu shower of silence

bathes you with a personalized hush,
with the individualized absence
of earfuls of tidings and tones.

Silence parcels its morsels
as bits of breezes felt by no one
but you, for a minute or two.

A prayer, a library, a garden, a mime,
Antarctica, the passing of time,
the soundless slap of a fish, bedtime,

all possess a dollop of silence, shared
by no other lull in the commotion
of matter in motion when cacophony cracks.

When my wife gave me the silent treatment,
my anger pulsed as a silent eruption.
I strolled the consummate calm of the woods

and attempted to reassemble the sea
of silence, but no two tiny ripples
fit together in the oceanic suspense.

Near the trees, a graveyard shrugged
and shivered its flags in agreement.
No tinkering can mend a void's fracture.

Then I gazed up into the vacuity of space.
Big decisions were once made way up there.
Silence can make you hear silent things.

LAKE OF THE WOODS

Our galaxy's grandest lake
masquerades as a woods.
Innumerable islands, secret nests, roost
in endless miles of circular shorelines
on Lake of the Woods.

Minnesotans are mavericks,
and this lake names their nature.
Even its acronym, LOW, broadcasts
its birthright, its timeless truths:
primitive, rudimentary, primeval.

In the state of ten thousand lakes,
this basin launched ten thousand isles.
Like tiny towns adrift in the water,
these boroughs embody a quest
for independence, for exalting their place

in Nature, in abundant clean water,
aside rugged winter-wise trees,
amongst the unfathomable depth of blue sky.
Rocky isles arose from submerged mountains,
seeking an airier acquaintance with rain.

Water flashes its beauty in raindrops,
and this lost liquid unravels

its flowing fabric as parcels of lake.
Just so, an island flaunts one scintilla
of land, an acre's shocking whisper.

A lake's persona arises from its shores
while water wavers, shifting its visage.
Find the lake's temperament, its identity,
strung on the fringes, rims, brim, and brink,
as a wreath, garlanding the sparkling wet world.

Find a glacial rock necklace, jewels
festooning the lake, a string of pearls
collaring the rippling realm, medallions
of antiquity, alive in their ancient age,
hard thoughts among the lake liquid's soft soul.

Find the lake's encircling crown
of trembling aspen, paper birch,
jack pine, spruce, oak, and balsam fir.
Spring's green gemstones shift
and revolve in flamboyant seasons.

Each queen of the forest flashes
her tiara, the trademark of her reign.
Every monarchy vanishes,
then resurges, resplendent as ever.
Lake waters sanction each ruler.

Upon misty mornings, gaze through the veil
hovering atop the LOW potions. Imagine each island

announces a castle. Find turrets and flags
in the towering pine, in the grandeur of the fir.
What hidden minions spring through the drawbridge!

Each island harbors its secrets,
much as do men. Reclusive rocks,
secluded, faraway, solitary outliers,
contemplate selfdom
and eccentricities of the neighbors.

Each island brandishes banners
of centuries past. Massacre Island
found ghastly fame when a Sioux
war party butchered a band
of voyageurs, in repose from canoeing.

On Sultana Island, the gold rush
dug shiny ore from the bedrock.
Today, glittering sand circles
the isle. Silica's scintillation
remains in lustrous allure.

Each island welcomed past guests.
Every visit bequeathed to the isle
one uncommon memory,
an aura wafting over lake waves,
the archival essence of singular sagas.

At sunset, on LOW, all matter and motion
cease commotion and comingle

and merge in symphonic silence,
the pause in the music. Storming hordes
of red brilliance fuse the sky, trees, and froth.

None witnessing this splendor will wish
to depart from the majestic finale
as Heaven's hand caresses the calmed lake.
The sky submerges. The tree line lingers,
blacker than night, then one with the water.

Each morning, a new world emerges,
so it seems, and the islands reappear
as huge stepping-stones for some giant
who follows the labyrinthine trail
on the lake's shimmering surface.

America's top hat, the Northwest Angle
totes this lake liquid, as if bottling
the bliss in a vast jar of indigenous wilds,
a saintly stratosphere at the top of a nation,
cloistered from the wicked abyss beyond.

Close your eyes. Taste Nature
as lake water wafts the rattling
of whirling repose and renewal.
A vibrant bouquet, dynamic, spry,
buoyant, bathes the jovial air.

Only one bird will speak at a time,
as though understood in this neighborhood

that each syllable ushers one blessed
conviction, one eccentric notion,
no other dispatch ever addressed.

The lake's trembling reflection
of a Christian cross, set atop
a lakeside church, manifests
Man's eternal bond with God,
as impetuous as a lake's shivers.

Sky and lake conspire to color
creation. When one begets blue,
so does its confederate—but never
identical blue. For lake blue ripples
in ruffles. Sky blue dodges its clouds,

as if these hazy specters
schemed to whitewash the canvas
of the lake, delicately designed
in infinitesimal dents reigning an instant,
then renouncing its prior contours.

When the clouds burn in volcanic
orange, the lake coat blushes,
a genial hearth, a mirage
cordially glowing in pastoral
grace, a place of aloof faith.

Imps tumble within the dimples
of the lake's surface. Press your hand

in the water and view the circling
waves expand. Water crawls always,
but chirps when caressed.

I fancied my hand captured the creature,
though each island bolted this beast
into its corral, its station in creation,
where this wonder fills before flight
to the firmament above, which pours

down rejuvenation, battalions of rain,
to replenish its northern flow
to Lake Winnipeg, a slippery stranger,
a friend of the family, an outlandish
outsider, engaged in exotic escapades.

Black shadows of clouds prowl
the tabletops of lakes. Minnesota
reigns as the Land of Leaks,
for her watersheds pour their potions
in motions north, south, west, and east.

Charter boats from Baudette and Warroad
ferry fishermen atop LOW's watery road.
Each angler gawks at the veneer of this vault,
mesmerized by the glints of the gemstones,
the dimples, nicks, and notches billowing,

shuddering, convulsing, rolling trillions
of ridges that rise and recede,

as petite liquid angels waving
their wings for an instant, then plunging
into the depths to rendezvous there.

Truly, Heaven's throne flashes its palace
in the mysterious milieu of LOW, lower
than the realm of the clouds, higher
than the timeworn crypts of Earth's cellar.
This ethereal liquor harbors a blest kingdom.

Jumbo perch patrol like archangels,
gliding fast as a figment. Smallmouth bass
descend as cherubim in deepwater.
Huge fearsome seraphim—muskies,
sturgeon, and pike—astonish mere men.

Of these bathing behemoths, one
beautiful beast, one lake fairy,
ascends as a legend, the immersed
gnome who illumes Minnesota's mien,
the submerged soul who construes

Northland mettle, the sage in the lake.
Some speak its name in a whisper, lest
casual banter affronts the hauteur
of this venerable kingpin, the veteran
elder of all factually fanciful lore.

Air dwellers christened it, "Walleye,"
an epithet announcing the twinned mirrors

bejeweling its angular head. A man's eye
preens as a window to the passion below.
Find in this fish the eyes of an abyss,

eyes seeming to not see you.
But look again! They see you too well.
Your sentience has entered their ghost eyes.
The light springing back from their retinal glass
emerges sifted and sieved, sorting your soul.

We sense that they see us, unfiltered,
and behold us as the authors of the annals
we actualize and abandon each day.
The lit lantern sprung from their eyes
glows so gloriously genuine, we revel

in the righteous portrayal of riddles
confounding each hour. In the depths
of these bottomless eyes, we find
redemption. Find yourself innocent,
blameless, for none can ever know his true self.

Walleye vision functions fantastically.
They prowl as dark water hunters,
in deep water by day. Dusk summons
them to murky shores where they feed
on the sleepy, those whose perception

falters in the gloom before dawn.
Much as do men, the walleyes

snatch opportunity from those
in habitual haunts, unschooled
in the risks and rewards of the pond.

No other fish flesh teases the tongue
as do walleye, the quintessential
lake lodger, the one fish whose flavor
bellows and boasts of our deepest domain.
Savor its sentience in a fish fry on shore.

Fish fail to shove the lake's water away,
with each twist of their torsos.
Just so, an ambience interns us,
from fetus to finality. Above all, none escape
from the sentry patrolling the brain basin.

In winter, LOW lays a fresh landscape.
Two thousand square miles of pavement
materialize magically. Two feet of ice
coat the lake liquid below. A new nation
emerges over the hidden fluidity.

Walk on the water. Drive a tractor atop
the new planet arisen from itself,
as though mother and child endured birth
in the wild. No invaders raid this nameless nation.
No new towns make a mark on the map.

The sparkling ice forewarns of the furnace
traversing the sky. The newborn terrain

might remain. But every known chronicle portends
a transient vista. The lid on the lake allots
wooly migrants a season of fresh avenues.

Only ice fishermen's houses rise on the rink.
Frigid anglers drill holes through the barrier.
Some imagine they open the portal to Heaven,
where the freshwater oracle awaits. They seek news
from the lake sprite with ghostly mirrored eyes.

SNOW PLANET

Tumbling and traveling gravity's rails,
tatters of ice imps, unfurling their sails,
flurry right past.
Stratosphere's cast
flee a cloud's blast,
hovering haltingly, tattling their tales.

Snowflakes' descension, revolving in air,
launches a jailbreak. None stroll the same stair,
humming their song,
loitering long,
flaunting their throng,
baring their piety packed in a prayer.

Numberless avenues spanning the sky
chaperone singular sprites as they fly,
meandering slow,
stop and then go.
Vagabond snow
relishes vistas these sightseers spy.

Breezes, exhaling tumultuous tracks,
ruffle the riders with wind at their backs.
Flakes never know
floors in the show,

hidden below.
Clouds only stuff prima donnas in sacks.

Ivory discs of brief thoughts flutter down.
Remnants of reveries ripped from the gown
grapple the breeze,
leaping in ease,
flouting the freeze.
Solitaire, fugitive flakes seek renown.

Blankets of comrades now litter the ground.
All had sought freedom, but all are found bound.
Clouds upon grass
lie in a mass,
pawns of their class,
rebels of governance caged in a mound.

Plowing machinery then hummed on the road.
Savage galactic moon lander, it mowed
drifts from the streets.
Thirty-inch sheets
ceded defeats.
Snow planets will loathly forgo their abode.

Silently, snowfall recaptured its reign.
Shoeprints once planted no longer remain.
Ghosts now abide.
They and I hide,
access denied,
living outside the domain of the brain.

Plows never found me, encased in the lake.
Delicate coatings of ice won't forsake
vagrants who stride
clouds, with no guide.
On their last ride,
flakes on a frolic will wander and wake.

BOUNDARY WATERS CANOE AREA, MINNESOTA

At the boundary of silence, a hushed colossus
of Nature pauses the passage of time.
One candle dazzles its castle. The blue hue

of its palace, arisen to a heavenly dome,
bathes in waters below, as though,
an invisible mist, between, unseen,

wanders as a wilderness rumor, a specter
sprung from lost generations of evergreen
graves. Leafy glows ruffle the shores,

trembling as emerald phantoms, in precarious
pondering, restless but reticent to pledge
allegiance to the genial chaos of Nature.

When steamy vapors dance upon waters,
the wavering portraits of trees softly simmer,
preparing to plunge into the rippling mirror.

Each sunset surprises the sheltered tranquility.
A galaxy's fire roars inaudibly, flashing
the mayhem of red, its ethos, its pith.

The fading flames aggrandize the harmony
of this pristine otherworld, never known
by avid guests who solely savor its crust.

The waters mutter, lapping the shores,
as a loon carols psalms of the wild,
and winds whisk the depths of a boreal forest.

No map marks the blessed site of wandering
solitude. A legion of isles naps in the lakes,
as dots detached from a dream.

ABOUT THE AUTHOR

Hari Hyde is also the author of *The Honeygate Chronicles*, a satirical, fantasy adventure trilogy. Many readers who loved the lyrical style of those fables forecast Hari Hyde's pilgrimage into poetry. Following *Unbathed Brains: Poems from Minnesota and the Milky Way*, Hari's new poetry collection recounts smalltown Minnesota and the glorious wilderness that abides in the North Star State, and in his own uncharted state of mind. Dr. Hyde, a farm boy, grew up near Middle River, Minnesota, and although he has traveled the world, he never really left his hometown.

Made in the USA
Middletown, DE
22 December 2024